GO PROGRAMMING FOR

ABSOLUTE BEGINNERS

LEARN THE BASICS AND START CODING

CONFIDENTLY

SIMON TELLIER

Table of Contents

CHAPTER 1: INTRODUCTION TO GO PROGRAMMING

1.1 What is Go?

Go, often referred to as Golang, is a statically typed, compiled programming language designed by Google to be simple, efficient, and powerful. It was created in 2007 by Robert Griesemer, Rob Pike, and Ken Thompson, three engineers at Google, who wanted to solve the complexities of large-scale software development. Go was officially announced to the public in 2009, and since then, it has rapidly gained popularity among developers.

At its core, Go was designed to address some of the shortcomings of other programming languages in handling modern software development needs. It offers a blend of the speed and efficiency of low-level languages like C and C++, combined with the simplicity and productivity of high-level languages like Python and JavaScript. This makes Go a great choice for developers working on scalable systems, cloud services, web applications, networking, and other high-performance applications.

What sets Go apart is its simplicity. While many programming languages have grown complex over time, Go was built to keep things straightforward. It avoids excessive features, focusing instead on delivering what developers need: fast compilation, clear and concise syntax, and easy-to-understand code. It doesn't have an overwhelming set of features or libraries, but it does offer everything required to build high-performance applications without unnecessary overhead.

Go's syntax is clean, with minimalistic design choices, which means developers can spend more time solving problems and less time worrying about language quirks.

Additionally, it's designed with concurrency in mind, offering powerful features like goroutines and channels, which make it easier to write programs that can run multiple tasks simultaneously. This is particularly useful in modern computing, where scalability and parallelism are essential for efficient applications.

The Go compiler is incredibly fast, meaning developers can quickly compile their programs and test their changes. Its efficiency also extends to memory management, where Go's garbage collector helps manage memory without putting a burden on the developer.

Another notable feature of Go is its strong support for interfaces and composition over inheritance, which promotes a more modular and flexible approach to designing software. With Go, you can easily build maintainable and scalable systems without having to dive into the complexities of object-oriented programming or excessive boilerplate code.

In addition to its simplicity and performance, Go is also cross-platform, meaning you can write Go programs on one system and run them on various operating systems, such as Windows, macOS, and Linux, without needing significant changes to the code. This makes it an attractive option for developers working on diverse platforms and environments.

Whether you are building a small command-line tool or a large, distributed system, Go's combination of speed, simplicity, and concurrency makes it a language that can handle a wide range of programming challenges.

1.2 Why Learn Go?

There are plenty of reasons why learning Go is a valuable investment, whether you are a beginner programmer or an experienced developer. Its rise in popularity in recent years, particularly among companies that deal with large-scale web services and cloud computing, has made it one of the most in-demand programming languages in the industry. Below are some of the key reasons why learning Go can give you a competitive edge in today's software development landscape.

1. Simplicity and Efficiency

One of the primary reasons to learn Go is its simplicity. Unlike other languages, Go was designed to keep things as simple as possible while still being powerful enough to tackle complex tasks. Its syntax is minimal, which reduces the learning curve for new developers and increases productivity for seasoned programmers. Go does away with a lot of the boilerplate code found in other languages, letting you write cleaner and more maintainable programs. This makes it an excellent choice for beginners who want to learn programming without feeling overwhelmed by language-specific complexities.

At the same time, Go remains highly efficient, both in terms of execution and development time. Programs written in Go run quickly and are well-optimized for performance. Go's compilation is fast, and its runtime is incredibly efficient, even when managing memory through its garbage collection system. This makes Go a go-to language for developers who need to build high-performance applications, without sacrificing simplicity in their code.

2. Strong Concurrency Support

Another standout feature of Go is its concurrency model. Concurrency is the ability for a program to execute multiple tasks at the same time, and it's essential in modern software development. Whether you're working on web servers, cloud-based systems, or
3

data-processing applications, concurrent programming helps maximize performance and responsiveness.

In Go, concurrency is a first-class citizen. The language provides goroutines, which allow functions to run concurrently in the background with minimal overhead. Goroutines are lightweight and do not require a significant amount of system resources, making it easy to scale applications. Go also offers channels, which allow goroutines to communicate and synchronize with each other. This means you can easily build programs that execute multiple tasks simultaneously without worrying about managing complex threads or race conditions. This makes Go a powerful tool for building scalable, high-performance applications, particularly in areas like microservices, web servers, and real-time systems.

3. Wide Industry Adoption
Go's popularity is not just a trend; it's a language that many major companies and organizations rely on. Some of the biggest names in the tech industry, including Google, Uber, Dropbox, Docker, and many more, use Go extensively in their software infrastructure. Google, in particular, has built several major internal systems with Go, including their massive cloud infrastructure.

Because of its speed, simplicity, and scalability, Go has become the language of choice for cloud-based services, web development, and microservices architecture. Learning Go opens up career opportunities in these fields, as companies actively seek developers who can write efficient, concurrent code.

4. A Growing Ecosystem
Go has a rapidly growing ecosystem of libraries, frameworks, and tools that make it easier to build applications in various domains, from web development and network programming to data analysis and cloud computing. The Go community is active and

welcoming, and there are plenty of resources available to help you learn and grow as a Go developer.

For instance, Go has excellent support for web frameworks such as Gin and Echo, and libraries for handling JSON, XML, and other formats, making it a fantastic choice for web and API development. The Go community also actively contributes to a wide array of open-source projects, which you can leverage in your own projects.

Moreover, Go's simplicity means that it is easy to read and maintain open-source libraries and frameworks. Whether you are contributing to a project or using an existing one, Go's clear syntax makes it easy to understand and modify.

5. Job Opportunities and Demand

As more companies embrace Go for their back-end and infrastructure needs, the demand for Go developers continues to grow. Whether you're looking to work in cloud computing, microservices, web development, or data systems, learning Go gives you access to a wide range of career opportunities.

Job listings for Go developers are on the rise, with roles available for entry-level, intermediate, and senior developers. Go developers can expect to earn competitive salaries, especially if they specialize in areas such as cloud infrastructure, containerization (e.g., Kubernetes, Docker), or distributed systems.

6. A Strong Community and Learning Resources

Learning Go is easier than ever, thanks to the strong community and wealth of resources available to new and experienced developers alike. The Go community is known for being friendly, helpful, and eager to share knowledge. There are numerous forums, tutorials, and online courses where you can find guidance and support.

Additionally, Go's official documentation is extensive and well-maintained, providing clear explanations and examples for all aspects of the language. There are also plenty of free resources, including blog posts, YouTube tutorials, and open-source projects, that make learning Go accessible to everyone.

7. Versatility in Use Cases

Go is a versatile language that can be used in a wide range of applications. From building web servers and APIs to developing distributed systems and working with cloud technologies, Go is capable of handling many types of tasks.

Whether you're building a small command-line tool or a large, complex system, Go offers the tools and features necessary to handle the job. It is especially useful in systems programming, microservices architecture, networking, and cloud computing, making it a great choice for modern software development.

8. Excellent Documentation and Support

Go's official documentation is one of the best in the industry. It's comprehensive, easy to navigate, and continuously updated. The Go community provides ample support through forums, GitHub repositories, Stack Overflow, and other platforms where developers can ask questions and get help.

For developers who prefer self-paced learning, Go also has interactive tutorials available, helping beginners quickly grasp the fundamentals. Moreover, Go's simplicity and clean syntax mean that even when you're working independently, you're unlikely to get bogged down by confusion over language specifics.

Learning Go means investing in a programming language that not only offers speed and simplicity but also provides the tools necessary for modern software development.

Whether you're working on backend systems, web applications, or cloud computing, Go's focus on concurrency, performance, and ease of use makes it an ideal language to learn and master. In the following chapters, we will dive deeper into Go's syntax, features, and practical applications, helping you build the confidence to start writing your own Go programs.

1.3 Setting Up Your Go Environment

Before you can start writing and running Go programs, you'll need to set up your development environment. Fortunately, Go's setup process is straightforward and involves only a few steps. In this section, we'll guide you through installing Go on your system, setting up your workspace, and preparing everything you need to start coding.

Step 1: Install Go

The first step is to install Go on your computer. Go is available for various operating systems, including Windows, macOS, and Linux. Here's how you can install it on each platform:

- **For Windows**:
    1. Go to the official Go downloads page: https://golang.org/dl/
    2. Download the Windows installer (.msi) file.
    3. Run the installer and follow the prompts. The default installation directory is usually fine.
    4. Once installed, Go will automatically add itself to your system's PATH, so you can run Go commands directly from the command prompt.
    5. Verify the installation by opening the command prompt and typing go version. If everything is installed correctly, you should see the Go version printed in the terminal.

- **For macOS**:
    1. Download the .pkg installer for macOS from the official Go downloads page.
    2. Open the downloaded file and follow the installation instructions.
    3. Once installed, Go should be added to your system's PATH.
    4. You can check the installation by opening a terminal window and typing go version.
- **For Linux**:
    1. The easiest way to install Go on Linux is by downloading the binary distribution from the official Go downloads page.

Extract the archive to /usr/local (or another location you prefer):

bash

Copy

```
tar -C /usr/local -xzf go1.x.linux-amd64.tar.gz
```

    2. Add /usr/local/go/bin to your PATH environment variable by editing your .bashrc or .bash_profile:

ruby

Copy

```
export PATH=$PATH:/usr/local/go/bin
```

    3. Reload the shell or run source ~/.bashrc to apply the changes.
    4. Check if Go is installed by typing go version in the terminal.

Step 2: Set Up Your Go Workspace

Go uses a workspace structure to organize your code. While Go doesn't strictly require a workspace setup (you can work without one), using the workspace makes it easier to manage your projects.

- The Go workspace consists of three main directories:
    - src (source code): This is where your Go source files will reside.
    - pkg (compiled package files): This directory stores the compiled packages.
    - bin (executables): This directory is where Go places any compiled executables.

To create a Go workspace, follow these steps:

Create a directory to store your Go projects. This directory will be your workspace. For example, create a folder named go_projects:

bash

Copy

mkdir ~/go_projects

1. Inside your workspace, create the src, pkg, and bin directories:

    javascript

    Copy

    mkdir ~/go_projects/src ~/go_projects/pkg ~/go_projects/bin

2. Next, set the GOPATH environment variable to point to this workspace. On Windows, you can set this via the Environment Variables panel. On macOS or Linux, add the following to your .bashrc or .bash_profile:

    bash

Copy

export GOPATH=$HOME/go_projects

export PATH=$PATH:$GOPATH/bin

3. Reload your shell or run source ~/.bashrc to apply the changes.

Step 3: Verify the Installation

To verify that Go is installed and the workspace is set up correctly, you can use the go env command in your terminal. This will print out details of your Go environment, including your GOPATH and other important paths. If everything is set up correctly, you should see the correct paths listed.

Now that you've installed Go and set up your workspace, you're ready to start coding!

1.4 Your First Go Program: "Hello, World!"

Now that your environment is ready, let's dive into writing your first Go program. We'll start with the classic "Hello, World!" program, which is a great way to ensure everything is working correctly and to get a feel for how Go syntax looks.

Step 1: Create a New Go File

1. Open your terminal and navigate to the src directory in your Go workspace (or any project directory where you want to create your code).

Create a new file called hello.go. You can do this by running the following command:

bash

Copy

touch hello.go

2. Open the hello.go file in your preferred text editor.

Step 2: Write the Code

In the hello.go file, type the following Go code:

go
Copy
```go
package main

import "fmt"

func main() {
    fmt.Println("Hello, World!")
}
```

Let's break this down:

- package main: This defines the package name. Every Go program must have a main package, which is where the execution of the program starts.
- import "fmt": This imports the fmt package, which contains functions for formatted I/O. In this case, we're using it to print text to the console.
- func main(): This defines the main function, which is the entry point of every Go program. It's where the program starts executing.
- fmt.Println("Hello, World!"): This line prints the string "Hello, World!" to the console.

Step 3: Run the Program

Now that you've written the code, it's time to run your program. To do this, open the terminal and navigate to the directory where hello.go is saved. Then, run the following command:

go
Copy
go run hello.go

This command tells Go to compile and run the hello.go file. You should see the following output:

Copy
Hello, World!

Congratulations! You've just written and run your first Go program.

1.5 How to Write, Run, and Debug Go Code

Writing Go code is straightforward, but understanding how to run and debug your code effectively is crucial to becoming proficient in the language. In this section, we'll cover the basics of writing, running, and debugging Go code.

Writing Go Code

Writing Go code is similar to writing code in many other programming languages. The syntax is simple, and Go encourages good coding practices by discouraging unnecessary complexity. You'll typically create a .go file, write your code inside the main function or other functions, and then use the go run or go build commands to execute your code.

Here's a simple structure for a Go program:

go
Copy

```
package main

import "fmt"

// Define a function
func greet(name string) {
    fmt.Println("Hello,", name)
}

func main() {
    // Call the greet function
    greet("Alice")
}
```

In this program, the greet function is defined to print a greeting message. It is then called from the main function with the argument "Alice". To run this program, simply use go run filename.go.

Running Go Code

There are two main ways to execute Go code:

go run: This command compiles and runs the Go program in one step. It's perfect for quick tests and small programs.

go

Copy

```
go run filename.go
```

1. go build: This command compiles the Go program into an executable file. This is useful when you want to compile your program and run it later, or distribute the compiled binary.

   go

   Copy

   ```
   go build filename.go
   ```

This creates an executable file in your current directory (on Windows, it will be filename.exe). You can then run the program by typing:

csharp

Copy

```
./filename (on macOS/Linux)
filename.exe (on Windows)
```

Debugging Go Code

Debugging is an essential part of the development process. While Go does not have an integrated debugger built into the language itself, there are a few common strategies for debugging Go programs.

14

- **Using Print Statements**: The simplest way to debug Go code is by adding fmt.Println() statements at various points in your program to check the values of variables or track program flow. While this isn't the most efficient way to debug, it can be helpful for quickly identifying problems.

Using a Debugger: Go supports integration with debuggers such as delve. Delve is a powerful debugger for Go that allows you to set breakpoints, inspect variables, and step through code. To use delve, install it using the following command:

go

Copy

```
go install github.com/go-delve/delve/cmd/dlv@latest
```

Once installed, you can start a debugging session by running:

go

Copy

```
dlv debug filename.go
```

With dlv, you can set breakpoints, inspect the state of your program, and step through each line of code, making it much easier to track down bugs.

Common Errors in Go

- **Syntax Errors**: These are common in any programming language and occur when you write code that doesn't follow the language's syntax rules. Go is a statically typed language, which means it checks for errors at compile time, helping you catch issues early.
- **Nil Pointer Dereference**: This error happens when you try to access a value or method of a nil pointer. Always ensure your pointers are properly initialized before using them.

15

- **Unresolved Imports**: If you forget to import a required package or if there's a typo in the import statement, Go will throw an error saying it can't find the package.

By understanding the basics of how to write, run, and debug your Go programs, you'll be able to quickly identify and fix issues, making your development process more efficient. As you grow more familiar with Go, you'll find that debugging and testing become natural parts of the coding workflow.

Chapter 2: Understanding Go Basics

2.1 Introduction to Variables and Constants

One of the fundamental concepts in any programming language is how to store and manipulate data. In Go, this is done using **variables** and **constants**. Understanding how to declare and use them is essential to writing effective Go programs.

What Are Variables?

A variable in Go is a storage location with a name that holds a value. The value of a variable can change (hence the term "variable"). Variables are used to store data, which can be of different types, such as numbers, strings, or booleans.

Declaring and Initializing Variables

There are a few ways to declare and initialize variables in Go. The most common ways are:

Using the var keyword: The var keyword allows you to declare a variable and optionally assign it a value. If you don't assign a value immediately, Go will assign a default zero value based on the variable's type.

go
Copy
```
var name string
var age int
var isActive bool
```

1. In the example above, we've declared three variables: name (a string), age (an integer), and isActive (a boolean). Since we didn't assign any values, Go

17

automatically sets them to their zero values ("" for strings, 0 for integers, and false for booleans).

Declaring and initializing variables in one line: You can also declare a variable and assign a value to it in one line.

go

Copy

```
var name string = "Alice"
var age int = 30
```

2. Here, we're declaring the name and age variables and initializing them with the values "Alice" and 30, respectively.

Using short variable declarations: Go allows you to declare and initialize a variable using the := shorthand syntax. This is useful when the type can be inferred from the value you assign.

go

Copy

```
name := "Alice"
age := 30
```

3. In this case, Go automatically figures out that name is a string and age is an integer based on the values we assign to them. The := syntax can only be used inside functions (it doesn't work at the package level).

Variable Types and Zero Values

In Go, every variable has a specific type, which determines the kind of data it can store (e.g., an integer, a string, a boolean). When you declare a variable but don't explicitly assign a value, Go assigns a **zero value** to the variable based on its type. This ensures that the variable always has a valid, predictable value.

Here are some common zero values in Go:

- 0 for numeric types (e.g., int, float32)
- false for booleans
- "" (empty string) for strings
- nil for pointers, channels, and function types

Changing the Value of a Variable

Once a variable is declared and initialized, you can change its value as needed.

```go
Copy
age := 30
age = 31
fmt.Println(age) // Output: 31
```

In this example, the variable age was initially set to 30, but we later updated it to 31.

What Are Constants?

A **constant** in Go is similar to a variable, except that its value cannot be changed after it's set. Constants are useful when you need to ensure that a value remains constant throughout the execution of your program.

You can declare a constant using the const keyword, followed by the name of the constant, its type (optional), and its value.

19

go

Copy

```
const Pi float64 = 3.14159
const Greeting = "Hello, World!"
```

In the example above, Pi is a constant of type float64, and Greeting is a constant string. The type for Greeting is inferred by Go because we assigned a string value to it.

Constants are typically used for values that should remain unchanged, such as mathematical constants, configuration values, or flags that don't change during the program's execution.

Summary:

- Variables are used to store values that can change, while constants are used for values that cannot change.
- You can declare and initialize variables using the var keyword or the short variable declaration syntax (:=).
- Go automatically assigns zero values to uninitialized variables.
- Constants are declared using the const keyword and cannot be modified once assigned a value.

2.2 Data Types: Numbers, Strings, and Booleans

In Go, data types specify what kind of value a variable can hold. Go is a **statically typed language**, meaning that the type of a variable is known at compile time. In this section, we'll explore the most commonly used data types: **numbers**, **strings**, and **booleans**.

Numbers in Go

Go supports both **integer** and **floating-point** numbers. Integer numbers represent whole numbers, while floating-point numbers represent decimal values.

1. **Integer Types**: Go provides a few different integer types, with varying sizes:
   - int and uint: These are the most commonly used integer types, and their size depends on the platform (usually 32-bit or 64-bit). For most applications, you can use int unless you specifically need unsigned integers or fixed-size integers.
   - int8, int16, int32, int64: These are signed integer types with specific sizes (8, 16, 32, and 64 bits, respectively).
   - uint8, uint16, uint32, uint64: These are unsigned integer types, which can store only positive values and zero. They have the same sizes as their signed counterparts.

Example:

go

Copy

```
var a int = 42
var b uint = 100
var c int64 = -1000000
```

   - a is a signed integer with the default int type, b is an unsigned integer (uint), and c is a 64-bit signed integer.

2. **Floating-Point Types**: Go also provides two floating-point types:
   - float32: A 32-bit floating-point number.
   - float64: A 64-bit floating-point number. This is the default type for floating-point numbers in Go, and it offers more precision than float32.

Example:

go

Copy

```
var pi float64 = 3.14159
var temperature float32 = 98.6
```

     o pi is a float64, and temperature is a float32.

Complex Numbers: Go also supports **complex numbers**, which consist of both a real and imaginary part. You can use the complex64 and complex128 types to represent complex numbers.

Example:

go

Copy

```
var z complex128 = complex(3, 4)
fmt.Println(z) // Output: (3+4i)
```

Strings in Go

A **string** is a sequence of characters enclosed in double quotes ("). Strings in Go are immutable, which means that once a string is created, it cannot be changed. However, you can create new strings based on operations on existing ones.

Strings are represented as UTF-8 encoded data, which allows them to store any character from virtually any language.

Example:

go

Copy

```
var name string = "Alice"
```

```go
var message = "Hello, " + name + "!"
fmt.Println(message) // Output: Hello, Alice!
```

In this example, we've created a string name and then concatenated it with another string to form the message "Hello, Alice!".

You can also get the length of a string using the len() function:

go
Copy
```go
fmt.Println(len(name)) // Output: 5
```

Booleans in Go

A **boolean** in Go can hold one of two values: true or false. Booleans are often used in conditional statements and loops to control the flow of a program.

Example:

go
Copy
```go
var isActive bool = true
if isActive {
    fmt.Println("The user is active.")
} else {
    fmt.Println("The user is not active.")
}
```

In this example, the program checks the value of isActive and prints the corresponding message based on whether it's true or false.

Summary of Data Types:

- **Numbers**: Go supports integer types (int, int8, int16, int32, int64, uint8, uint16, uint32, uini64) and floating-point types (float32, float64).
- **Strings**: A sequence of characters represented as UTF-8 encoded text. Strings in Go are immutable.
- **Booleans**: Can be true or false, used for conditional logic.

By understanding and utilizing these basic data types, you'll be able to write more complex and useful Go programs. As you continue learning, you'll encounter additional data types and structures, such as arrays, slices, and structs, which will allow you to organize your data even more efficiently.

2.3 Using Operators in Go

Operators are an essential part of any programming language, allowing you to manipulate and evaluate values. Go supports a wide range of operators that enable you to perform arithmetic, comparison, logical, and other operations. In this section, we'll explore the various types of operators you can use in Go.

Arithmetic Operators

Go supports the basic arithmetic operators commonly found in most programming languages, including addition, subtraction, multiplication, division, and modulus.

- + (Addition): Adds two values.
- - (Subtraction): Subtracts one value from another.

- * (Multiplication): Multiplies two values.
- / (Division): Divides one value by another (for integer division, Go uses integer truncation).
- % (Modulus): Returns the remainder of division.

Example:

go
Copy
```
a := 10
b := 5

fmt.Println(a + b) // Output: 15
fmt.Println(a - b) // Output: 5
fmt.Println(a * b) // Output: 50
fmt.Println(a / b) // Output: 2
fmt.Println(a % b) // Output: 0
```

Comparison Operators

Comparison operators are used to compare two values and return a boolean result (true or false).

- == (Equal to): Returns true if the values are equal.
- != (Not equal to): Returns true if the values are not equal.
- > (Greater than): Returns true if the left value is greater than the right.
- < (Less than): Returns true if the left value is less than the right.

- >= (Greater than or equal to): Returns true if the left value is greater than or equal to the right.
- <= (Less than or equal to): Returns true if the left value is less than or equal to the right.

Example:

go
Copy

```
a := 10
b := 5

fmt.Println(a == b)  // Output: false
fmt.Println(a != b)  // Output: true
fmt.Println(a > b)   // Output: true
fmt.Println(a < b)   // Output: false
fmt.Println(a >= b)  // Output: true
fmt.Println(a <= b)  // Output: false
```

Logical Operators

Logical operators are used to combine multiple boolean expressions. Go supports the following logical operators:

- && (AND): Returns true if both operands are true.
- || (OR): Returns true if at least one operand is true.
- ! (NOT): Reverses the boolean value of its operand.

Example:

```go
Copy
a := true
b := false

fmt.Println(a && b) // Output: false
fmt.Println(a || b) // Output: true
fmt.Println(!a)     // Output: false
```

Assignment Operators

Assignment operators are used to assign values to variables. In addition to the basic = operator, Go also supports compound assignment operators that combine arithmetic operations with assignment.

- =: Assigns the value on the right to the variable on the left.
- +=: Adds the right value to the left variable and assigns the result to the left variable.
- -=: Subtracts the right value from the left variable and assigns the result to the left variable.
- *=: Multiplies the left variable by the right value and assigns the result to the left variable.
- /=: Divides the left variable by the right value and assigns the result to the left variable.
- %=: Applies the modulus operation to the left variable using the right value.

27

Example:

go
Copy
```
a := 10
a += 5  // a = a + 5
fmt.Println(a)  // Output: 15

a *= 2  // a = a * 2
fmt.Println(a)  // Output: 30
```

Increment and Decrement Operators

Go uses ++ for incrementing a variable by 1, and -- for decrementing it by 1. These operators can be used in both pre- and post-increment/decrement forms.

- ++ (Increment): Increases the value of the variable by 1.
- -- (Decrement): Decreases the value of the variable by 1.

Example:

go
Copy
```
a := 10
a++
fmt.Println(a)  // Output: 11

a--
fmt.Println(a)  // Output: 10
```
28

Bitwise Operators

Bitwise operators are used to manipulate the individual bits of integer values. Go supports the following bitwise operators:

- &: AND operation
- |: OR operation
- ^: XOR operation
- &^: AND NOT operation
- <<: Left shift
- >>: Right shift

Example:

go
Copy
```
a := 5   // 0101 in binary
b := 3   // 0011 in binary

fmt.Println(a & b)  // Output: 1 (0001 in binary)
fmt.Println(a | b)  // Output: 7 (0111 in binary)
fmt.Println(a ^ b)  // Output: 6 (0110 in binary)
```

Summary:

- Go supports arithmetic, comparison, logical, assignment, increment/decrement, and bitwise operators.

- Arithmetic operators perform basic mathematical operations, while comparison operators are used to compare values.
- Logical operators combine boolean values, and assignment operators help assign values to variables.
- Bitwise operators allow manipulation of integer values at the bit level.

2.4 Control Flow: Conditionals (if, else, switch)

In Go, **conditional statements** allow you to control the flow of execution based on specific conditions. These conditions are typically boolean expressions that evaluate to true or false. Go provides the if, else, and switch statements for handling these conditions.

if Statement

The if statement is used to execute a block of code if a specified condition is true. It can be followed by an else block to execute code when the condition is false.

Syntax:

go
Copy

```
if condition {
    // code to be executed if condition is true
}
```

You can also use an else block to handle the case when the condition is false:

go
Copy

```go
if condition {
    // code to be executed if condition is true
} else {
    // code to be executed if condition is false
}
```

Example:

go
Copy
```go
a := 10
if a > 5 {
    fmt.Println("a is greater than 5")
} else {
    fmt.Println("a is not greater than 5")
}
```

In this example, since a is 10, the program will print "a is greater than 5."

else if Statement

You can chain multiple conditions together using else if to check for more than one condition.

Syntax:

go
Copy

31

```
if condition1 {
    // code for condition1
} else if condition2 {
    // code for condition2
} else {
    // code if neither condition is true
}
```

Example:

go
Copy

```
a := 10
if a > 20 {
    fmt.Println("a is greater than 20")
} else if a > 5 {
    fmt.Println("a is greater than 5 but less than or equal to 20")
} else {
    fmt.Println("a is less than or equal to 5")
}
```

Here, the output will be "a is greater than 5 but less than or equal to 20."

switch Statement

The switch statement is a more concise way to handle multiple conditions that might otherwise require many if-else blocks. It checks a variable against several possible values, executing the block of code corresponding to the first match.

Syntax:

go
Copy
```
switch expression {
case value1:
    // code to be executed if expression == value1
case value2:
    // code to be executed if expression == value2
default:
    // code to be executed if no case matches
}
```

Example:

go
Copy
```
day := "Monday"

switch day {
case "Monday":
    fmt.Println("Start of the workweek")
```

```go
case "Friday":
    fmt.Println("Almost the weekend!")
default:
    fmt.Println("Midweek")
}
```

In this case, the program will output "Start of the workweek."

The switch statement can also evaluate boolean expressions directly:

go
Copy
```go
a := 10

switch {
case a > 5:
    fmt.Println("a is greater than 5")
case a < 5:
    fmt.Println("a is less than 5")
default:
    fmt.Println("a is equal to 5")
}
```

Summary:

- The if statement executes a block of code if a condition is true, with an optional else block for the false case.
- You can chain multiple conditions with else if.

- The switch statement allows for concise handling of multiple possible conditions.
- Switch can be used with expressions or boolean conditions for more flexible logic.

2.5 Loops: for Loop and Infinite Loops

Loops are an essential control structure in any programming language, enabling you to repeat a block of code multiple times. Go provides a single loop construct, the for loop, which can be used for a wide range of looping tasks, including infinite loops.

The for Loop

The for loop in Go is the only loop construct you need. It is versatile and can be used in several different ways, depending on the scenario.

Basic syntax:

go
Copy
```
for initialization; condition; post {
    // code to be executed
}
```

1. **For loop with initialization, condition, and post statement**:
   o The initialization part is executed once before the loop starts.
   o The condition is checked before each iteration. If it evaluates to true, the loop executes.

o The post statement is executed after each iteration (usually used to update loop variables).

Example:

go
Copy
```
for i := 0; i < 5; i++ {
    fmt.Println(i)
}
```

This loop will print the numbers from 0 to 4.

2. **For loop with just a condition (while loop)**: You can omit the initialization and post statements, making the for loop function like a while loop.

Example:

go
Copy
```
i := 0
for i < 5 {
    fmt.Println(i)
    i++
}
```

This will also print the numbers from 0 to 4.

3. **Infinite Loops**: By omitting both the condition and post statements, you can create an infinite loop that will run indefinitely.

Example:

go
Copy

```
for {
    fmt.Println("This will run forever!")
}
```

To stop an infinite loop, you typically use a break statement, which terminates the loop

- The for loop is the only loop construct in Go but is extremely flexible.
- It can be used like a while loop or as a traditional for loop.
- Go also supports infinite loops, but you should use a break statement to exit them when necessary.

Chapter 3: Functions in Go

3.1 What Are Functions?

Functions are a fundamental building block of Go (and most programming languages). A **function** is a block of code that performs a specific task and can be reused throughout a program. By organizing code into functions, you can break down complex tasks into smaller, more manageable pieces. Functions help make your code more modular, reusable, and easier to understand.

In Go, a function consists of two main parts:

1. **A function signature**, which includes the function's name, parameters, and return type(s).
2. **The function body**, which contains the code that defines what the function does when it is called.

The main purpose of using functions is to group together logic that performs a specific task and can be reused, making your code more organized, readable, and maintainable.

Functions can have:

- **Zero or more parameters** (values passed to the function when it is called).
- **Zero or more return values** (values returned from the function when it finishes executing).

Function Benefits:

- **Modularity**: Functions allow you to write one section of code and call it in different parts of your program, avoiding duplication.

- **Abstraction**: You can hide the complexity of certain tasks behind a function, exposing only the necessary details.
- **Reusability**: A well-written function can be reused in multiple places, which saves time and reduces the chance of errors.
- **Testing**: Functions make it easier to test specific pieces of functionality in isolation.

Let's look at how functions are declared and how they work in Go.

3.2 Defining and Calling Functions

In Go, functions are declared using the func keyword. A function definition includes its name, parameters, return type(s), and the code block inside the function.

Basic Syntax:

```go
Copy
func functionName(parameter1 type, parameter2 type) returnType {
    // function body
    // code to execute
    return returnValue
}
```

Here's a breakdown of the syntax:

- func: This keyword marks the beginning of a function definition.
- functionName: The name of the function. This should be a descriptive name that reflects the task the function performs.

39

- parameter1 type, parameter2 type: These are the parameters passed into the function. Each parameter has a name and a type. You can have zero or more parameters.
- returnType: The type of value the function returns. A function can return a single value, multiple values, or no value at all.
- return returnValue: The return statement specifies the value that is returned from the function. If a function does not return anything, this is omitted.

Example:

Let's define a simple function in Go that adds two integers and returns the sum.

go
Copy

```go
func add(a int, b int) int {
    sum := a + b
    return sum
}
```

In this function:

- add is the function name.
- a and b are the parameters of type int.
- The function returns an int, which is the result of adding a and b.

Calling Functions

Once a function is defined, you can call it from anywhere in your code (as long as it's in scope). To call a function, you use its name followed by parentheses containing the arguments (the values to pass to the parameters).

Example:

go
Copy

```
func main() {
    result := add(3, 4) // Call the add function with arguments 3 and 4
    fmt.Println(result)  // Output: 7
}
```

In the main function, we call the add function with the arguments 3 and 4. The function adds them together and returns the result, which we store in the variable result. We then print the result, which is 7.

Multiple Return Values

One powerful feature of Go functions is the ability to return multiple values. Go allows functions to return more than one value, which can be useful for cases like error handling, returning multiple results, or working with complex data.

To return multiple values, simply specify them in the function definition and use a tuple-like return syntax.

Example:

go
Copy
```go
func divide(a int, b int) (int, int) {
    quotient := a / b
    remainder := a % b
    return quotient, remainder
}
```

In this function, we are dividing a by b and returning both the quotient and the remainder.

Calling a Function with Multiple Returns:

go
Copy
```go
func main() {
    q, r := divide(10, 3)
    fmt.Println("Quotient:", q) // Output: Quotient: 3
    fmt.Println("Remainder:", r) // Output: Remainder: 1
}
```

Here, the function divide is called with the arguments 10 and 3. It returns two values, which we capture in the variables q and r. We then print both values.

If you don't need one of the returned values, you can use the blank identifier _ to discard it.

42

Example:

go

Copy

```go
func main() {
    q, _ := divide(10, 3)
    fmt.Println("Quotient:", q) // Output: Quotient: 3
}
```

In this example, we only care about the quotient, so we discard the remainder using _.

Named Return Values

You can also name the return values in a function declaration. This can make your code more readable and allows you to return values without using the return statement explicitly.

Example:

go

Copy

```go
func divide(a int, b int) (quotient int, remainder int) {
    quotient = a / b
    remainder = a % b
    return
}
```

43

Here, quotient and remainder are named return values. In the function body, we assign values to these variables and then use a bare return, which implicitly returns the named values.

Variadic Functions

Go also supports **variadic functions**, which can take a variable number of arguments. This is useful when you don't know in advance how many arguments will be passed to the function.

A variadic function is declared using ... before the type of the parameter.

Example:

go
Copy
```go
func sum(nums ...int) int {
    total := 0
    for _, num := range nums {
        total += num
    }
    return total
}
```

In this example, nums is a variadic parameter that allows the function to accept any number of integers. Inside the function, we iterate over nums and sum the values.

Calling a Variadic Function:

```go
func main() {
    result := sum(1, 2, 3, 4, 5)
    fmt.Println(result) // Output: 15
}
```

You can pass any number of arguments to the sum function, and it will return their total.

- Functions in Go are defined using the func keyword.
- Functions can accept parameters and return values.
- Go supports multiple return values and variadic functions (functions that accept a variable number of arguments).
- You can also define **named return values** to simplify code and avoid explicitly using the return keyword in the body.
- Functions are essential for organizing and reusing code.

Understanding how to define and call functions will help you write efficient, modular Go programs that are easier to maintain and extend.

3.3 Function Parameters and Return Values

Function parameters and return values are essential parts of Go functions. They allow you to pass data into functions for processing and return results. Understanding how to work with function parameters and return values will help you write more flexible and powerful Go programs.

Function Parameters

When defining a function, you can specify parameters that accept values from the caller. These parameters allow you to customize the behavior of the function depending on the input. In Go, parameters are defined with a name followed by its type.

A function can have zero, one, or more parameters. The number and types of parameters in the function definition determine how you pass data into the function.

Basic Example:

go

Copy

```go
func greet(name string) {

    fmt.Println("Hello, " + name)

}
```

In this example, the function greet accepts one parameter name of type string. When you call this function, you pass a string value to it, which it then prints.

Multiple Parameters

Functions in Go can also accept multiple parameters. When you declare multiple parameters, you separate each one with a comma.

46

go

Copy

```go
func add(a int, b int) int {

    return a + b

}
```

Here, the function add accepts two int parameters and returns their sum.

Omitting Types in Consecutive Parameters

Go allows you to omit the type for all but the last parameter in a series of parameters, making the code slightly more concise.

go

Copy

```go
func add(a, b int) int {

    return a + b

}
```

In this case, both a and b are of type int, so we only specify the type for the last parameter.

47

Named Parameters

You can also give names to function parameters, which can improve code readability. This makes the code more descriptive, especially in cases where the function has several parameters.

go

Copy

```go
func divide(a, b int) (quotient, remainder int) {

    quotient = a / b

    remainder = a % b

    return

}
```

In this example, quotient and remainder are named return values, and the parameters a and b are also clearly named.

Return Values

Go functions can return one or more values. The return value(s) are specified in the function signature after the parameters, and the function must use the return keyword to send the result(s) back to the caller.

A function can return:

- **Single return value**: If you only need to return one result.
- **Multiple return values**: Go allows functions to return more than one value. This is useful when you need to return multiple pieces of data, such as a result and an error.

Single Return Value Example:

go

Copy

```go
func square(x int) int {

    return x * x

}
```

Here, square takes one integer parameter and returns the square of that number.

Multiple Return Values Example:

go

Copy

```go
func divide(a, b int) (int, int) {

    quotient := a / b
```

```
    remainder := a % b

    return quotient, remainder

}
```

In this case, the divide function returns two values: the quotient and the remainder.

When calling a function that returns multiple values, you can capture them in variables:

go

Copy

```
quotient, remainder := divide(10, 3)

fmt.Println(quotient, remainder) // Output: 3 1
```

If you are only interested in one return value, you can use the blank identifier _ to discard the other:

go

Copy

```
quotient, _ := divide(10, 3)

fmt.Println(quotient) // Output: 3
```

Summary:

- Function parameters allow you to pass data to a function.
- Functions can return one or more values.

50

- Parameters and return values must have types, and Go supports both single and multiple return values.

3.4 Variable Scope and Function Scope

In Go, the scope of a variable determines where in the program the variable can be accessed. Understanding variable scope is crucial to avoid naming conflicts and to write efficient code.

What is Scope?

- **Global Scope**: Variables declared outside of all functions are in the global scope. These variables are accessible throughout the entire program.
- **Local Scope**: Variables declared within a function are in the local scope. They are only accessible within that function.

Global Scope

In Go, you can declare a variable outside of any function, which makes it accessible to all functions in the package. These are known as **global variables**. However, using global variables should be avoided unless necessary, as they can make code harder to maintain and understand.

Example:

go

Copy

```
package main
```

```go
import "fmt"

var globalVar = "I am global"

func printGlobalVar() {

    fmt.Println(globalVar) // Accessing the global variable

}

func main() {

    printGlobalVar()

}
```

Here, globalVar is declared outside any function, so it is accessible inside the printGlobalVar function.

Local Scope

Variables declared inside a function are only accessible within that function. These are known as **local variables**. They cannot be accessed by other functions outside their scope.

Example:

go

Copy

```go
func main() {
```

```go
    var localVar = "I am local"

    fmt.Println(localVar)  // This works because we're inside the same function

}


// The following will cause an error because localVar is out of scope

// fmt.Println(localVar)
```

In this case, localVar is only accessible within the main function. Trying to access it outside the function would result in a compilation error.

Block Scope

Go also supports block-level scope, meaning that variables declared inside loops, conditionals, or other code blocks are limited to that block.

Example:

go

Copy

```go
func main() {

    if true {

        var blockVar = "I am block scoped"
```

```go
        fmt.Println(blockVar)  // This works

    }

    fmt.Println(blockVar)  // Error: blockVar is not defined outside the block

}
```

In this example, blockVar is only accessible within the if block. Trying to access it outside that block will result in an error.

Shadowing Variables

Variable shadowing occurs when a local variable has the same name as a variable in an outer scope. In this case, the inner variable "shadows" the outer variable, and the inner variable takes precedence within its scope.

Example:

go

Copy

```go
package main


import "fmt"
```

54

```go
var x = 10  // Global variable

func main() {

    x := 20  // Local variable

    fmt.Println(x)  // Output: 20, because the local variable shadows the global one

}
```

Here, the local variable x inside the main function shadows the global variable x. The program will print 20 because the local variable takes precedence inside the main function.

Summary:

- Variables have either global or local scope.
- Global variables are accessible throughout the program, while local variables are confined to the function or block where they are declared.
- Go supports block-level scope and allows variable shadowing, which can lead to bugs if not handled carefully.

3.5 Anonymous Functions and Closures

In Go, **anonymous functions** are functions that are defined without a name. They are often used when you need a quick, one-off function for a specific task. These functions are also known as **lambdas** or **function literals**.

Anonymous Functions

You can define an anonymous function inline and execute it immediately or assign it to a variable for later use. Anonymous functions are commonly used when you want to pass a function as an argument to another function or return a function from another function.

Example:

go

Copy

```go
func main() {
    // Defining and calling an anonymous function
    func() {
        fmt.Println("Hello from an anonymous function!")
    }()


    // Assigning an anonymous function to a variable
    greet := func(name string) {
        fmt.Println("Hello, " + name)
    }
```

```
greet("Alice")

}
```

In this example:

- The first anonymous function is defined and called immediately inside the main function.
- The second anonymous function is assigned to the variable greet and called later with the argument "Alice".

Closures

A **closure** is a function that captures and remembers the variables from the surrounding scope in which it was defined. In Go, closures allow you to create functions that have access to variables even after the scope in which they were created has finished executing.

A closure "remembers" the environment in which it was created, and it can access and modify the variables from that environment even when called outside of that environment.

Example:

go

Copy

```
func main() {
```

```go
counter := 0

// Anonymous function that captures the counter variable

increment := func() int {

    counter++

    return counter

}

fmt.Println(increment()) // Output: 1

fmt.Println(increment()) // Output: 2

}
```

In this example, the increment function is a closure that captures and modifies the counter variable from the surrounding scope. Each time increment() is called, it remembers and updates the value of counter.

- **Anonymous functions** are functions without a name, used for quick tasks or passed as arguments.
- **Closures** are functions that capture and remember variables from their surrounding scope, allowing them to maintain state across calls.

- Go's support for anonymous functions and closures enables more flexible and powerful programming techniques, such as passing functions as arguments or creating custom functions on the fly.

Chapter 4: Working with Data Structures

4.1 Introduction to Arrays

Arrays are one of the fundamental data structures in Go and many other programming languages. An array in Go is a fixed-size collection of elements of the same type. Arrays are useful when you know the exact number of elements you will need to store and don't need to resize the collection during the program's execution.

Declaring Arrays in Go

To declare an array in Go, you specify the type of elements it will hold and its size. The syntax is:

```go
Copy
var arrayName [size]Type
```

- arrayName is the name of the array.
- [size] is the number of elements the array can hold.
- Type is the data type of the elements.

For example, to declare an array of 5 integers, you can do:

```go
Copy
var numbers [5]int
```

This creates an array named numbers that can hold 5 integers. By default, all elements in an array are initialized to the zero value for their type. For integers, this value is 0.

Initializing Arrays

You can initialize an array with specific values at the time of declaration. There are two main ways to initialize arrays in Go:

1. **Using explicit values**:

go
Copy
```
var numbers = [5]int{1, 2, 3, 4, 5}
```

This creates an array of integers with 5 elements, where each element is initialized with the values 1, 2, 3, 4, and 5.

2. **Using an ellipsis (...) to infer the size**:

go
Copy
```
numbers := [...]int{1, 2, 3, 4, 5}
```

In this case, Go automatically determines the size of the array based on the number of elements in the initializer.

61

Accessing and Modifying Array Elements

You can access and modify array elements using an index. Go uses zero-based indexing, meaning the first element of the array is at index 0, the second at index 1, and so on.

go
Copy

```go
numbers := [5]int{1, 2, 3, 4, 5}

// Accessing an element
fmt.Println(numbers[0]) // Output: 1

// Modifying an element
numbers[1] = 10
fmt.Println(numbers[1]) // Output: 10
```

Array Length

To get the length of an array, you use the len() function, which returns the number of elements in the array.

go
Copy

```go
fmt.Println(len(numbers)) // Output: 5
```

Arrays Are Fixed-Size

One important characteristic of arrays in Go is that they are **fixed-size**. Once you declare an array with a specific size, you cannot change the size of the array later. If you need a collection with a dynamic size, Go provides the slice type, which we will cover in the next section.

Example of Using Arrays:

go
Copy
```
package main

import "fmt"

func main() {
    var numbers [5]int = [5]int{1, 2, 3, 4, 5}

    fmt.Println("Array elements:")
    for i := 0; i < len(numbers); i++ {
        fmt.Println(numbers[i])
    }
}
```

In this example, we loop through the array and print each element. The len(numbers) gives the size of the array, which is 5 in this case.

Multidimensional Arrays

Go also supports multidimensional arrays, which are arrays of arrays. A two-dimensional array can be thought of as a matrix or table with rows and columns.

go
Copy
```go
var matrix [2][3]int
matrix[0][0] = 1
matrix[0][1] = 2
matrix[0][2] = 3
matrix[1][0] = 4
matrix[1][1] = 5
matrix[1][2] = 6

fmt.Println(matrix)
```

This example creates a 2x3 array (2 rows and 3 columns) and initializes its elements. The output will be:

lua
Copy
```lua
[[1 2 3] [4 5 6]]
```

Summary of Arrays:

- Arrays in Go are fixed-size collections of elements of the same type.
- The size of an array is part of its type, and arrays are zero-indexed.

64

- You can initialize arrays with explicit values or let Go infer the size with the ... syntax.
- Arrays are useful when you know the exact number of elements you need and don't require resizing.

4.2 Slices: A Dynamic Array

While arrays are useful in certain cases, they are not flexible enough for many real-world applications, as their size is fixed once defined. To address this limitation, Go provides **slices**, a more flexible and dynamic alternative to arrays.

What is a Slice?

A **slice** is a dynamically-sized, flexible view into an array. Unlike arrays, slices can grow and shrink in size as needed, which makes them far more useful in situations where the size of the collection may change during the execution of a program.

Slices provide an abstraction over arrays, allowing you to work with portions of an array or even whole arrays without worrying about their fixed size.

Declaring and Initializing Slices

You can declare a slice in Go in several ways, similar to arrays, but without specifying the size. Go automatically manages the slice's size internally.

1. **Declaring an empty slice:**

go
Copy

65

```go
var numbers []int
fmt.Println(numbers) // Output: []
```

Here, numbers is an empty slice, and its length is 0.

2. Creating a slice with make():

Go provides the make() function to create slices with a specified length and capacity. The capacity determines how much space the slice can grow before it needs to be reallocated.

go
Copy
```go
numbers := make([]int, 5)  // A slice of 5 integers, with zero values
fmt.Println(numbers) // Output: [0 0 0 0 0]
```

In this case, numbers is a slice with 5 elements, each initialized to the zero value for integers (0).

3. Creating a slice from an array:

You can create a slice from an existing array or another slice using a slicing operation.

go
Copy
```go
arr := [5]int{1, 2, 3, 4, 5}
slice := arr[1:4]  // This creates a slice with elements from index 1 to index 3
fmt.Println(slice)  // Output: [2 3 4]
```

This creates a slice that includes the elements of the array arr from index 1 to index 3 (note that the ending index is exclusive).

4. **Using the [] syntax to create a slice**:

go
Copy
```
numbers := []int{1, 2, 3, 4, 5}
fmt.Println(numbers) // Output: [1 2 3 4 5]
```

This creates a slice directly from a list of values. It's equivalent to creating an array, but the size of the slice is automatically determined.

Accessing and Modifying Slice Elements

Just like arrays, you can access and modify elements of a slice using zero-based indexing.

go
Copy
```
slice := []int{1, 2, 3, 4, 5}
fmt.Println(slice[0])  // Output: 1

slice[2] = 10
fmt.Println(slice)  // Output: [1 2 10 4 5]
```

67

Slice Length and Capacity

Slices have two important properties: **length** and **capacity**.

- **Length**: The length of a slice is the number of elements it contains. You can get the length of a slice using the len() function.
- **Capacity**: The capacity of a slice is the number of elements the slice can hold before it needs to be resized. You can get the capacity of a slice using the cap() function.

go

Copy

```go
numbers := make([]int, 5, 10) // Length = 5, Capacity = 10
fmt.Println(len(numbers)) // Output: 5
fmt.Println(cap(numbers)) // Output: 10
```

Appends and Resizing Slices

One of the key advantages of slices over arrays is that they can be dynamically resized. You can append new elements to a slice using the built-in append() function.

go

Copy

```go
numbers := []int{1, 2, 3}
numbers = append(numbers, 4) // Append a single element
fmt.Println(numbers) // Output: [1 2 3 4]

numbers = append(numbers, 5, 6) // Append multiple elements
fmt.Println(numbers) // Output: [1 2 3 4 5 6]
```

68

The append() function creates a new slice if the original slice does not have enough capacity to hold the new elements. Go takes care of allocating a new array and copying the old elements into it, so you don't have to manage that manually.

Copying Slices

Go provides the copy() function to copy one slice into another. The copy() function copies elements from the source slice to the destination slice.

```go
Copy
source := []int{1, 2, 3, 4}
destination := make([]int, 4)
copy(destination, source)
fmt.Println(destination) // Output: [1 2 3 4]
```

If the destination slice has more elements than the source slice, the extra elements are not changed. If the destination slice is smaller, only as many elements as it can hold are copied.

Summary of Slices:

- A **slice** is a flexible, dynamically-sized collection that can grow and shrink as needed.
- You can create a slice using make(), by slicing an existing array, or by using the [] syntax.
- Slices have both a **length** (the number of elements) and a **capacity** (the number of elements the slice can hold before needing to be resized).

- The append() function allows you to add elements to a slice, and copy() enables you to copy one slice into another.

Slices are incredibly powerful and flexible and should be your go-to data structure when working with collections that might change in size. Unlike arrays, slices provide the dynamic resizing capabilities that are common in many modern programming languages.

4.3 Maps: Key-Value Pairs

In Go, a **map** is an unordered collection of key-value pairs. Maps are similar to hash tables or dictionaries in other programming languages. They provide a fast way to look up values based on a key, making them an essential tool for storing and accessing data efficiently.

Declaring and Initializing Maps

To declare a map in Go, you use the make() function or the map literal syntax. The key type and value type must be specified when creating the map.

1. **Using make() to create a map**:

go
Copy
```
m := make(map[string]int)
```

This creates an empty map m with string keys and integer values. Initially, the map has no entries.

70

2. **Using map literals:**

You can initialize a map with predefined key-value pairs using map literals:

```go
Copy
m := map[string]int{"Alice": 25, "Bob": 30}
```

This creates a map with two key-value pairs: "Alice": 25 and "Bob": 30.

Adding and Modifying Entries in a Map

To add a key-value pair to a map or modify the value associated with an existing key, you simply assign the value to the key:

```go
Copy
m := make(map[string]int)
m["Alice"] = 25
m["Bob"] = 30
fmt.Println(m)  // Output: map[Alice:25 Bob:30]
```

If you assign a value to an existing key, the value is updated.

Accessing Values in a Map

To retrieve the value associated with a key, you use the key inside square brackets:

```go
Copy
age := m["Alice"]
```

71

```go
fmt.Println(age)  // Output: 25
```

If the key is not found in the map, Go returns the zero value for the value type (e.g., 0 for integers).

Checking if a Key Exists in a Map

Go provides a way to check if a key exists in a map using a second value in the assignment expression. If the key is found, the second value will be true; otherwise, it will be false.

go
Copy
```go
age, exists := m["Bob"]
if exists {
    fmt.Println("Bob's age is", age)
} else {
    fmt.Println("Bob is not in the map")
}
```

In this example, if "Bob" exists in the map, the program prints "Bob's age is 30". If "Bob" is not in the map, the program prints "Bob is not in the map".

Deleting Entries in a Map

You can remove an entry from a map using the delete() function:

go
Copy

72

```go
delete(m, "Bob")
fmt.Println(m)  // Output: map[Alice:25]
```

The delete() function removes the key-value pair associated with the key "Bob" from the map.

Maps with Different Key and Value Types

Maps in Go can store keys and values of any type, but some types are not allowed as map keys, such as slices, maps, and functions. Keys must be of a type that supports equality comparisons, such as integers, strings, or pointers.

Example:

```go
go
Copy
m := make(map[int]string)
m[1] = "One"
m[2] = "Two"
fmt.Println(m[1])  // Output: One
```

Summary of Maps:

- Maps in Go store key-value pairs, where each key maps to a value.
- You can declare maps using make() or map literals.
- You can add, retrieve, modify, and delete key-value pairs in a map.
- You can check for the existence of a key using the second return value from a map lookup.

4.4 Structs: Defining Custom Data Types

A **struct** in Go is a composite data type that groups together variables (fields) under one name. Each field in a struct can have a different type, and structs are useful for representing real-world entities like a Person, Car, or Book.

Structs are analogous to classes in object-oriented programming but do not include methods or inheritance. Instead, Go provides a simple way to group related data into one entity.

Declaring and Initializing Structs

To declare a struct, you define the struct type and its fields. A struct's fields are defined with a name and a type. Here's an example:

go
Copy
```
type Person struct {
    Name string
    Age  int
}
```

This defines a Person struct with two fields: Name (of type string) and Age (of type int).

To create an instance of a struct, you can either initialize it with named fields or use the default zero values for all fields:

1. **Using named fields**:

go
Copy
```
person := Person{Name: "Alice", Age: 25}
fmt.Println(person) // Output: {Alice 25}
```

2. **Using default zero values**:

go
Copy
```
person := Person{}
fmt.Println(person) // Output: { 0}
```

In the second example, Name will have the zero value of an empty string (""), and Age will have the zero value of 0.

Accessing and Modifying Struct Fields

You can access and modify the fields of a struct using the dot (.) operator:

go
Copy
```
fmt.Println(person.Name) // Output: Alice
person.Age = 30
fmt.Println(person.Age)  // Output: 30
```

Pointer to a Struct

You can also create a pointer to a struct, which allows you to modify the struct's fields directly. Go passes structs by value, which means that copying a struct can be costly. Using pointers is an efficient way to avoid unnecessary copying of large structs.

go

Copy

```go
personPtr := &person  // Get a pointer to person
personPtr.Age = 35    // Modify the Age field through the pointer
fmt.Println(person.Age) // Output: 35
```

Anonymous Structs

Go allows you to define structs without giving them a type name. These are called **anonymous structs** and are often used for temporary or ad-hoc data structures.

go

Copy

```go
person := struct {
    Name string
    Age  int
}{
    Name: "Bob",
    Age:  40,
}
fmt.Println(person) // Output: {Bob 40}
```

Methods with Structs

In Go, methods can be associated with structs. These methods allow you to perform operations on a struct, similar to how you would define methods on objects in object-oriented languages.

To define a method on a struct, you specify the receiver type in the method declaration. The receiver can either be a value or a pointer to a struct.

```go
Copy
type Person struct {
    Name string
    Age  int
}

// Method with value receiver
func (p Person) Greet() {
    fmt.Println("Hello, my name is", p.Name)
}

// Method with pointer receiver
func (p *Person) CelebrateBirthday() {
    p.Age++
}

func main() {
    person := Person{Name: "Alice", Age: 25}
```

```go
    person.Greet()  // Output: Hello, my name is Alice
    person.CelebrateBirthday()
    fmt.Println(person.Age)  // Output: 26
}
```

In this example, Greet is a method with a value receiver, and CelebrateBirthday is a method with a pointer receiver.

Summary of Structs:

- Structs are custom data types that group related variables (fields) together.
- Fields in a struct can have different types.
- You can define methods on structs to perform operations on them.
- Go supports both value and pointer receivers for methods.

4.5 Arrays, Slices, and Maps in Action

Now that we've covered arrays, slices, and maps in detail, let's see how these data structures can be used together in a real-world example. We'll create a simple program that uses arrays, slices, and maps to track the scores of students in a class.

Example:

Let's consider a scenario where we have a class of students, and we need to store and manipulate their scores.

go
Copy

```go
package main

import "fmt"

type Student struct {
    Name  string
    Scores []int
}

func main() {
    // Create an array of Student structs
    students := [3]Student{
        {Name: "Alice", Scores: []int{85, 90, 88}},
        {Name: "Bob", Scores: []int{78, 82, 80}},
        {Name: "Charlie", Scores: []int{92, 95, 90}},
    }

    // Use a map to store the average scores for each student
    averages := make(map[string]float64)

    // Calculate average score for each student
    for _, student := range students {
        total := 0
        for _, score := range student.Scores {
            total += score
        }
        average := float64(total) / float64(len(student.Scores))
```

```
    averages[student.Name] = average
  }

  // Print the results
  for name, average := range averages {
      fmt.Printf("%s's average score: %.2f\n", name, average)
  }
}
```

In this example:

- We define a Student struct with fields for Name and Scores.
- We create an array of Student structs, each containing a name and a slice of scores.
- We use a map averages to store the average score for each student, using the student's name as the key.
- The program calculates the average score for each student and prints the results.

Output:

rust

Copy

```
Alice's average score: 87.67
Bob's average score: 80.00
Charlie's average score: 92.33
```

- **Arrays** are useful when you know the exact number of elements, but they have a fixed size.

80

- **Slices** are more flexible and can dynamically grow and shrink in size.
- **Maps** allow you to store data in key-value pairs, providing an efficient way to look up values based on keys.
- By combining these data structures, you can easily model and manipulate complex data in Go programs.

Chapter 5: Handling Errors and Debugging

5.1 The Importance of Error Handling

Error handling is an essential part of writing reliable and robust programs. In Go, error handling is explicit, meaning the programmer is responsible for handling errors directly instead of relying on exceptions or hidden mechanisms. This approach promotes clarity and ensures that errors are addressed and understood rather than silently ignored.

Why Error Handling Is Important

Errors are inevitable in most programs. Whether it's due to incorrect user input, network failure, or problems with reading or writing files, errors can occur at any point during the program's execution. If errors aren't handled correctly, they can lead to undefined behavior, program crashes, or unexpected results. Proper error handling ensures that your program behaves predictably even in the face of failures.

In Go, errors are treated as first-class values. Instead of throwing exceptions or using try-catch blocks, Go provides a way to return errors explicitly, allowing the caller to handle them in a controlled manner.

Error Handling in Go

In Go, the standard way to handle errors is by returning an error type from functions that may encounter an issue. Go's error type is a built-in interface, defined as:

go

Copy

```
type error interface {
    Error() string
```

}

Any type that implements the Error() method is considered an error type. This method returns a string message describing the error, which can then be used for debugging or logging.

Explicit Error Handling

Instead of relying on a hidden exception system, Go requires you to explicitly check for errors returned by functions that can fail. This makes error handling clear and explicit.

For example, when working with I/O operations like reading from a file, you may encounter an error if the file doesn't exist or if there's a problem with permissions. In Go, the os.Open() function returns both a file handle and an error, allowing you to check if something went wrong.

```go
Copy
package main

import (
    "fmt"
    "os"
)

func main() {
    file, err := os.Open("example.txt")
    if err != nil {
        fmt.Println("Error opening file:", err)
```

```
    return // Exit the function if there is an error
}
defer file.Close()

// Further file processing
fmt.Println("File opened successfully!")
}
```

In this example:

- os.Open("example.txt") attempts to open a file and returns two values: file (a file handle) and err (an error value).
- We explicitly check if err is not nil. If it is not nil, we know something went wrong, and we print the error and exit the function.
- If the file opens successfully, we continue processing.

Advantages of Explicit Error Handling

- **Clarity**: When errors are handled explicitly, it's clear where and why something failed. This makes the program more predictable and easier to understand.
- **Control**: Handling errors gives you control over what happens when an error occurs. You can decide whether to log the error, retry the operation, or terminate the program.
- **Maintainability**: Explicit error handling makes your code easier to maintain and debug because errors are addressed immediately instead of being hidden in the background.

Summary of Error Handling in Go:

- In Go, errors are treated as values and returned explicitly from functions that can fail.
- The error type is an interface that includes an Error() method, which provides a string message describing the error.
- Go requires the caller to check for errors explicitly, which makes error handling clear and predictable.

5.2 Returning Errors from Functions

In Go, functions that might encounter an error typically return an error value as the last return value. This allows the caller to check for errors after calling the function, providing the caller with the opportunity to decide how to handle the error.

Declaring Functions with Error Returns

When defining a function that can fail, you specify the error type as the last return value in the function's signature.

Here's a basic example:

```go
Copy
package main

import (
    "fmt"
```

```go
    "errors"
)

func divide(a, b int) (int, error) {
    if b == 0 {
        return 0, errors.New("division by zero") // Return an error if the denominator is
zero
    }
    return a / b, nil // No error, return the result and nil
}

func main() {
    result, err := divide(10, 0)
    if err != nil {
        fmt.Println("Error:", err) // Handle the error
        return
    }
    fmt.Println("Result:", result)
}
```

In this example, the divide function performs division and returns both the result and an error. If the denominator (b) is 0, the function returns an error with the message "division by zero". Otherwise, it returns the result of the division and nil for the error.

The error Type

The error type in Go is an interface that represents any type that has an Error() method. The errors package provides functions like errors.New() and fmt.Errorf() for creating error values.

- errors.New("message"): This creates a new error with the specified message.
- fmt.Errorf("message", args...): This creates a formatted error, similar to how fmt.Printf works, allowing you to create more complex error messages.

Example with fmt.Errorf()

```go
Copy
package main

import (
    "fmt"
    "errors"
)

func calculateDiscount(price float64, discountPercentage float64) (float64, error) {
    if discountPercentage < 0 || discountPercentage > 100 {
        return 0, fmt.Errorf("invalid discount percentage: %f", discountPercentage)
    }
    return price * (1 - discountPercentage/100), nil
}

func main() {
```

87

```
    price := 100.0
    discount := -10.0

    discountPrice, err := calculateDiscount(price, discount)
    if err != nil {
        fmt.Println("Error:", err)
        return
    }
    fmt.Println("Discounted price:", discountPrice)
}
```

In this case, we use fmt.Errorf to return a formatted error message when the discount percentage is invalid (less than 0 or greater than 100).

Custom Error Types

Go also allows you to create custom error types. This can be useful when you need more information about the error, such as an error code or additional context.

To create a custom error type, define a struct and implement the Error() method for that struct:

go
Copy
```
package main

import (
    "fmt"
```

```go
)

type FileError struct {
    Filename string
    Err      error
}

func (e *FileError) Error() string {
    return fmt.Sprintf("error with file %s: %v", e.Filename, e.Err)
}

func openFile(filename string) (string, error) {
    if filename == "" {
        return "", &FileError{Filename: filename, Err: fmt.Errorf("filename cannot be empty")}
    }
    return "file opened successfully", nil
}

func main() {
    result, err := openFile("")
    if err != nil {
        fmt.Println("Error:", err)
        return
    }
    fmt.Println(result)
}
```

In this example, we define a FileError struct with fields for the filename and the underlying error. The Error() method formats a custom error message. When the openFile function is called with an empty filename, it returns a FileError.

Error Handling Best Practices

- Always check for errors returned by functions, especially in critical sections of your code like file I/O, network requests, or user input validation.
- Return nil as the error value when the function succeeds. This is the Go convention.
- Provide meaningful error messages. A good error message helps others (and yourself) diagnose the problem quickly.
- If the error is recoverable (like invalid user input), handle it gracefully within the function. If it's not recoverable (like a failed network connection), return the error to the caller for them to handle.
- For complex applications, consider defining custom error types to carry additional context along with the error.

Summary of Returning Errors from Functions:

- Functions that can fail should return an error as the last return value.
- The error type is an interface that must implement the Error() method.
- You can create errors using errors.New() or fmt.Errorf().
- Custom error types can provide more context and useful information.
- Always check for errors and handle them appropriately.

Error handling in Go is explicit and essential to creating reliable programs. By returning errors from functions and checking them properly, you can ensure that your programs behave predictably, even in the face of unexpected conditions.

5.3 Using the "defer" Statement

The defer statement in Go allows you to schedule a function call to be executed **later**, just before the surrounding function returns. It is commonly used to ensure that resources are properly cleaned up (e.g., closing files, unlocking locks) even if an error occurs or if the function returns early.

How defer Works

When you use defer, the function call is not executed immediately but is deferred until the surrounding function completes. The deferred function call is executed in **LIFO (Last In, First Out)** order, meaning that the most recently deferred function is executed first.

Syntax:

go
Copy
```
defer functionName(arguments)
```

Example:

Here's an example that demonstrates the use of defer to ensure that a file is closed even if an error occurs during file operations.

go
Copy
```
package main
```

91

```go
import (
    "fmt"
    "os"
)

func openFile(filename string) (*os.File, error) {
    file, err := os.Open(filename)
    if err != nil {
        return nil, err
    }
    // Ensure that the file gets closed when we're done with it
    defer file.Close()

    // File operations here
    fmt.Println("File opened successfully")
    return file, nil
}

func main() {
    file, err := openFile("example.txt")
    if err != nil {
        fmt.Println("Error:", err)
        return
    }

    // Continue with the file operations
    fmt.Println(file.Name())
```

In this example:

- The openFile function opens a file and returns it.
- defer file.Close() ensures that the file will be closed when the function openFile returns, even if an error occurs in the file operations.

The key benefit here is that no matter what happens in the body of the openFile function, the Close() method will always be called before the function returns, preventing potential resource leaks.

Use Cases for defer

1. **Resource Cleanup (e.g., closing files, network connections)**:
   - Ensures that resources are released properly, even if an error occurs.
2. **Unlocking mutexes or other locks**:
   - Ensures that locks are released properly after acquiring them.
3. **Logging**:
   - You can use defer for logging purposes at the end of a function for easier debugging.
4. **Recovering from panics**:
   - You can use defer in combination with recover to catch panics and prevent your program from crashing.

Important Notes:

- defer statements are executed in **reverse order**, meaning the most recent one is executed first.

93

- Deferred functions will run even if the surrounding function has a return statement.

Summary of defer:

- defer is used to schedule function calls to be executed just before the surrounding function exits.
- It is typically used for cleaning up resources like files, locks, or network connections.
- defer ensures proper cleanup, even in cases where the function exits early due to an error.

5.4 Common Go Errors and How to Fix Them

In Go, errors can occur for a variety of reasons, from incorrect input to system failures (e.g., file not found, network issues). While Go's explicit error handling makes it easier to deal with errors, it's still important to understand common types of errors and how to resolve them effectively.

Common Go Errors and Their Fixes

1. **Nil Pointer Dereference**

One of the most common errors in Go is dereferencing a nil pointer, which leads to a runtime panic.

Example:

go
Copy
```
var ptr *int
fmt.Println(*ptr)  // Error: panic: runtime error: invalid memory address or nil pointer
dereference
```

Fix: Always check if a pointer is nil before dereferencing it.

go
Copy
```
var ptr *int
if ptr != nil {
    fmt.Println(*ptr)
} else {
    fmt.Println("Pointer is nil")
}
```

2. **Type Mismatch**

Go is a statically typed language, so type mismatches will result in compile-time errors. For example, trying to assign a string to an integer variable will produce an error.

Example:

go
Copy

```go
var x int
x = "hello"  // Error: cannot use "hello" (type string) as type int in assignment
```

Fix: Ensure that you are using the correct types for your variables. Perform explicit type conversions if necessary.

go

Copy

```go
var x int
x = 5  // Correct type assignment
```

3. Index Out of Range

Go provides an easy-to-use way to access elements in arrays, slices, and strings. However, trying to access an index outside of the bounds of these data structures will cause a runtime error.

Example:

go

Copy

```go
arr := []int{1, 2, 3}
fmt.Println(arr[5])  // Error: panic: runtime error: index out of range
```

Fix: Always ensure that you are accessing valid indices.

go

Copy

```go
arr := []int{1, 2, 3}
if index := 2; index < len(arr) {
```

96

```go
    fmt.Println(arr[index]) // Safe access
}
```

4. File Handling Errors

File handling operations like opening, reading, and writing files often return errors, such as "file not found" or "permission denied." These errors need to be checked explicitly.

Example:

go

Copy

```go
file, err := os.Open("nonexistent.txt")
if err != nil {
    fmt.Println("Error opening file:", err) // Error: panic if not handled
}
```

Fix: Always handle file errors explicitly and ensure you close the file after operations are complete.

go

Copy

```go
file, err := os.Open("existent.txt")
if err != nil {
    fmt.Println("Error opening file:", err)
    return
}
defer file.Close()
```

97

5. Concurrency Issues (Race Conditions)

When working with multiple goroutines, it's important to ensure that shared resources are accessed safely to avoid race conditions.

Example:

```go
Copy
var counter int

go func() {
    counter++
}()

go func() {
    counter++
}()
```

Fix: Use synchronization mechanisms like mutexes or channels to control access to shared resources.

```go
Copy
var counter int
var mu sync.Mutex

go func() {
```

98

```
    mu.Lock()
    counter++
    mu.Unlock()
}()

go func() {
    mu.Lock()
    counter++
    mu.Unlock()
}()
```

Summary of Common Errors and Fixes:

- **Nil Pointer Dereference**: Always check if a pointer is nil before dereferencing it.
- **Type Mismatch**: Ensure you use the correct types and perform explicit conversions when needed.
- **Index Out of Range**: Always validate array and slice indices before accessing them.
- **File Handling Errors**: Always check for errors when working with files and handle them properly.
- **Concurrency Issues**: Use synchronization techniques like mutexes to avoid race conditions.

5.5 Debugging Go Code: Tools and Techniques

Debugging is a critical part of the software development process. In Go, there are several tools and techniques available to help you debug and identify issues in your code.

1. Using Print Statements for Debugging

The simplest form of debugging is to insert fmt.Println() statements throughout your code to print values of variables and check program flow. This can be helpful for quickly checking the state of your program.

Example:

```go
Copy
fmt.Println("Starting the program")
fmt.Println("Variable value:", variable)
```

While effective for small programs, this method can become cumbersome in large codebases. Therefore, more advanced tools are often preferred for larger projects.

2. Go's Built-in Debugging Tools

Go comes with a built-in tool called **Delve** for interactive debugging. Delve allows you to inspect variables, set breakpoints, and step through your program's execution. It is a powerful tool for identifying issues at runtime.

Installing Delve: To install Delve, you can run:

100

bash

Copy

```
go install github.com/go-delve/delve/cmd/dlv@latest
```

Starting a Debugging Session: To start a debugging session with Delve, you can use the following command:

bash

Copy

```
dlv debug
```

This will start your Go program in a debugging environment. You can set breakpoints, step through the code, and examine variables.

3. Using Logs for Debugging

Logging is a more sophisticated version of using print statements. Rather than just printing output, you can use logging libraries to record information at different levels (e.g., info, debug, error).

The log package in Go is commonly used for logging:

go

Copy

```
import "log"

log.Println("Starting the process")
log.Printf("Processing item %d", itemID)
```

101

You can also use third-party logging libraries like logrus or zap for more advanced logging capabilities, such as logging to files, rotating logs, and structured logging.

4. Unit Testing and Test Coverage

Go has a built-in testing framework that allows you to write unit tests for your code. Unit tests help you identify bugs by testing individual components of your code in isolation. Writing comprehensive tests for your functions ensures that your code behaves as expected.

To run tests, use the go test command:

bash
Copy
```
go test
```

For test coverage analysis, use:

bash
Copy
```
go test -cover
```

This will provide a report on the test coverage of your code, helping you identify untested parts of your program.

5. IDE Debugging Tools

Many integrated development environments (IDEs) and editors, such as **Visual Studio Code** and **GoLand**, offer built-in debugging tools that integrate with Delve. These tools allow you to set breakpoints, step through code, and inspect variables directly within your editor, making debugging more efficient.

6. Profiling and Performance Analysis

Go includes the pprof package for profiling, which helps you understand where your program is spending most of its time. Profiling can be crucial for identifying performance bottlenecks.

You can generate a CPU profile by adding the following code to your program:

```go
Copy
import (
    "log"
    "os"
    "net/http"
    _ "net/http/pprof"
)

func main() {
    go func() {
        log.Println(http.ListenAndServe("localhost:6060", nil))
    }()
```

103

```
    // Your program's logic here
}
```

Then, you can use tools like go tool pprof to analyze the performance profile.

Summary of Debugging Techniques:

- **Print Statements**: Simple, but effective for small programs.
- **Delve**: A powerful interactive debugger for Go programs.
- **Logging**: A structured way to output debug information, often with log levels.
- **Unit Testing**: Use Go's built-in testing framework to write tests and catch bugs early.
- **IDE Tools**: Use IDEs with integrated debugging tools for a more efficient debugging experience.
- **Profiling**: Use Go's pprof package to analyze performance bottlenecks.

Debugging is a critical part of development, and Go provides a variety of tools and techniques to help you identify and fix issues. By using the right approach, you can ensure that your programs run smoothly and efficiently.

Chapter 6: Go's Concurrency Model

6.1 What is Concurrency in Programming?

Concurrency is the concept of performing multiple tasks or operations at the same time, but not necessarily simultaneously. The main goal of concurrency is to manage several tasks that could potentially run in parallel and utilize resources more efficiently. In the context of programming, it allows different parts of a program to be executed concurrently, which can improve performance, especially on modern multi-core processors.

Parallelism vs. Concurrency

While concurrency and parallelism are often used interchangeably, they are slightly different concepts:

- **Concurrency** is about dealing with multiple tasks at once, but these tasks may not necessarily run at the same time. A concurrent program can start tasks, pause them, and resume them in any order, giving the illusion of simultaneous execution. It is like multitasking where each task gets a slice of the CPU's time.
- **Parallelism**, on the other hand, refers to tasks that literally run simultaneously, often on different processors or cores. For parallelism to occur, the hardware must have multiple processing units (e.g., CPU cores) to execute the tasks at the

- same time.

Concurrency is more about structuring a program to handle multiple tasks efficiently, while parallelism is about executing those tasks at the same time, given the right hardware. Go allows you to write concurrent programs, and on multi-core systems, it can leverage parallelism to execute multiple tasks simultaneously.

Why Concurrency Matters

In modern applications, especially in web servers, network communication, and real-time systems, you often need to perform multiple tasks simultaneously. These tasks could include handling multiple user requests, processing data in the background, or waiting for input from different sources. Concurrency allows programs to efficiently manage these tasks, improving the overall responsiveness and throughput.

For example, imagine a web server that needs to handle thousands of incoming HTTP requests. Instead of handling them one after the other (which would be inefficient), the server can handle many requests at once, improving response times and throughput.

Concurrency in Go

Go provides an excellent concurrency model that is both simple and powerful. The Go concurrency model is built around two key concepts: **goroutines** and **channels**, which allow for communication and synchronization between concurrently executing tasks.

Go's concurrency model allows you to write concurrent programs without dealing with the complexities typically associated with concurrency, such as locking and thread management.

6.2 Goroutines: Introduction and Basic Usage

In Go, **goroutines** are the building blocks of concurrency. A **goroutine** is a lightweight thread of execution that is managed by the Go runtime. Goroutines allow you to run functions concurrently, without worrying about the low-level details of thread management. **What Are Goroutines?**

Goroutines are extremely lightweight compared to traditional threads. A goroutine is started by using the go keyword followed by a function call. The Go runtime multiplexes a small number of operating system threads onto many goroutines, allowing you to run thousands or even millions of goroutines concurrently.

The beauty of goroutines lies in their simplicity and efficiency. Unlike traditional threads, which can be heavy and expensive in terms of memory and CPU usage, goroutines are lightweight and managed by the Go runtime. This allows you to create highly concurrent applications without worrying about resource exhaustion.

Starting a Goroutine

To start a goroutine, you simply use the go keyword followed by a function or method call. Once a goroutine is started, it runs concurrently with the rest of the program, and the main function doesn't wait for the goroutine to finish unless explicitly instructed to.

Basic Example:

```
go
Copy
package main

import (
    "fmt"
    "time"
)
```

```
func sayHello() {
    fmt.Println("Hello from the goroutine!")
}
func main() {
    go sayHello()  // Start the sayHello function as a goroutine

    // The main function waits for 1 second to allow the goroutine to complete
    time.Sleep(time.Second)
    fmt.Println("Hello from the main function!")
}
```

In this example:

- The sayHello() function is started as a goroutine with the go keyword.
- The main() function continues running, but since we are not explicitly waiting for the goroutine to complete, we use time.Sleep() to ensure that the goroutine has enough time to print its message before the main function exits.
- The output is a mix of "Hello from the goroutine!" and "Hello from the main function!", showing that both run concurrently.

Key Characteristics of Goroutines:

1. **Lightweight**: Goroutines are much lighter than threads, allowing you to create thousands or millions of concurrent tasks without overwhelming your system.
2. **Independent Execution**: Each goroutine runs independently, so you don't need to explicitly manage their execution order.

3. **Managed by Go's Runtime**: The Go runtime manages the scheduling and execution of goroutines, efficiently multiplexing them across available CPU cores.
4. **Non-blocking**: Goroutines run independently and don't block the execution of the main program or other goroutines, unless you explicitly synchronize them using channels.

Using Goroutines with Functions

Goroutines can run any function concurrently. This makes it easy to perform tasks concurrently by just calling functions in parallel.

go
Copy

```go
package main

import "fmt"

func task1() {
    fmt.Println("Task 1 is running")
}

func task2() {
    fmt.Println("Task 2 is running")
}

func main() {
    go task1() // Start task1 as a goroutine
```

109

```
go task2()  // Start task2 as a goroutine

// Wait for both goroutines to finish
fmt.Scanln()  // Wait for user input (this allows the goroutines to finish)}
```

In this case, both task1 and task2 run concurrently in separate goroutines. The program doesn't terminate immediately because the main function waits for user input, giving both goroutines a chance to complete.

Goroutines and Concurrency

The go keyword is all you need to create concurrent operations in Go. Go's scheduler will manage when and how each goroutine runs. The underlying operating system threads may execute multiple goroutines concurrently, but you don't need to worry about managing those threads or their execution order.

The real power of goroutines lies in their ability to work together and share data. Goroutines can communicate with each other through **channels**, which we will cover later in this chapter.

Goroutines and the Go Runtime

The Go runtime manages the scheduling of goroutines. It runs on a pool of OS threads and assigns goroutines to these threads in an efficient manner. The Go scheduler uses a concept called **M:N scheduling** to multiplex many goroutines onto fewer OS threads.

- **M** represents the number of goroutines.
- **N** represents the number of OS threads.

The Go runtime schedules and assigns goroutines to threads as needed, and it adjusts the number of threads in use based on available CPU resources. This allows Go to handle large numbers of goroutines efficiently, without creating too much overhead.

Summary of Goroutines:

- Goroutines are lightweight concurrent units of execution in Go.
- They are started using the go keyword and run concurrently with the main program or other goroutines.
- Goroutines are managed by the Go runtime and are much more efficient than traditional threads.
- You can run any function concurrently by simply calling it in a goroutine, and the Go runtime handles scheduling and execution.

Go's concurrency model using goroutines is incredibly simple to use and powerful for writing highly concurrent applications. Goroutines are the foundation of Go's concurrency model and are essential for efficiently handling tasks that need to run in parallel, such as web servers, network processing, and background tasks. In the next section, we'll dive deeper into how to synchronize and communicate between goroutines using **channels**, a key feature of Go's concurrency model.

6.3 Channels: Communication Between Goroutines

In Go, **channels** are used to facilitate communication between goroutines. Channels allow goroutines to send and receive data safely, ensuring that information is passed between concurrent tasks without causing data races or inconsistencies. Channels are a key feature of Go's concurrency model, as they provide an elegant way to synchronize and communicate between multiple goroutines.

What is a Channel?

A **channel** is a data structure that allows one goroutine to send data to another goroutine. Channels are typed, meaning they can only carry data of a specific type. You can think of channels as a conduit through which goroutines pass data.

Declaring and Creating Channels

To declare a channel, you use the chan keyword followed by the type of data the channel will carry. You can create a channel using the make() function, specifying the type and optionally the capacity (buffered or unbuffered).

Unbuffered Channel (No capacity):

go
Copy
```
ch := make(chan int)
```

An **unbuffered channel** does not have any capacity, so sending data to the channel will block the sending goroutine until another goroutine receives the data from the channel.

Buffered Channel (With capacity):

go
Copy
```
ch := make(chan int, 3)
```

112

A **buffered channel** can hold a specific number of values (in this case, 3). Sending to a buffered channel will only block when the buffer is full, and receiving will block only when the buffer is empty.

Sending and Receiving Data from Channels

To send data to a channel, you use the <- operator:

go
Copy
```
ch <- value  // Send data to the channel
```

To receive data from a channel, you use the same <- operator but on the other side of the channel:

go
Copy
```
value := <-ch  // Receive data from the channel
```

Example of Using Channels:

go
Copy
```
package main

import "fmt"

func sendData(ch chan int) {
```

113

```go
    fmt.Println("Sending data...")
    ch <- 42  // Send data to the channel
}

func main() {
    ch := make(chan int)  // Create an unbuffered channel

    go sendData(ch)  // Start a goroutine to send data

    data := <-ch  // Receive the data from the channel
    fmt.Println("Received data:", data)
}
```

In this example:

- The sendData function sends the value 42 to the channel ch.
- The main function receives the data from the channel and prints it.
- Since the channel is unbuffered, the main goroutine waits for the data to be sent by the sendData goroutine before continuing.

Buffered vs. Unbuffered Channels

- **Unbuffered channels** provide synchronous communication between goroutines, meaning the sending goroutine waits for the receiving goroutine to receive the data.
- **Buffered channels** allow asynchronous communication, where sending and receiving can happen independently until the buffer is full or empty.

Closing Channels

A channel can be closed to indicate that no more data will be sent on it. Closing a channel is important for signaling to receiving goroutines that they should stop waiting for more data.

You can close a channel using the close() function:

```go
Copy
close(ch)
```

Once a channel is closed, no more values can be sent on it, but it's still possible to receive values until the channel is empty.

Example:

```go
Copy
package main

import "fmt"

func sendData(ch chan int) {
    for i := 0; i < 3; i++ {
        ch <- i
    }
    close(ch) // Close the channel after sending all data
}
```

115

```go
func main() {
    ch := make(chan int)

    go sendData(ch)

    // Receive data from the channel until it is closed
    for value := range ch {
        fmt.Println("Received:", value)
    }
}
```

In this example:

- The sendData function sends three values to the channel and then closes it.
- The main function uses a for loop with range to receive all values from the channel until it is closed.

Summary of Channels:

- Channels provide a way for goroutines to communicate and share data.
- You can create channels using the make() function and specify whether they are buffered or unbuffered.
- Data can be sent to and received from channels using the <- operator.
- Channels can be closed to indicate that no more data will be sent.

6.4 Select Statement for Concurrency Control

The select statement in Go provides a way to handle multiple channel operations simultaneously. It is similar to the switch statement, but instead of evaluating multiple expressions, the select statement evaluates multiple channel operations (send and receive).

The select statement is useful when you need to wait for multiple channel operations to complete, and it allows you to handle whichever channel operation happens first.

Syntax:

```go
Copy
select {
case channel1 <- value:  // Send data to channel1
    // Code to execute when the send operation on channel1 is successful
case value := <-channel2:  // Receive data from channel2
    // Code to execute when data is received from channel2
case <-time.After(time.Second):  // Timeout case
    // Code to execute when the timeout is reached
}
```

- Each case can represent a send or receive operation on a channel.
- The select statement will block until one of the cases is ready.
- You can also handle timeouts using time.After() or other non-blocking operations.

Example:

go

Copy

```go
package main

import (
    "fmt"
    "time"
)

func task1(ch chan string) {
    time.Sleep(2 * time.Second)
    ch <- "Task 1 completed"
}

func task2(ch chan string) {
    time.Sleep(1 * time.Second)
    ch <- "Task 2 completed"
}

func main() {
    ch1 := make(chan string)
    ch2 := make(chan string)

    go task1(ch1)
    go task2(ch2)
```

```go
// Use select to wait for the first task to complete
select {
case result := <-ch1:
    fmt.Println(result) // Output: Task 1 completed
case result := <-ch2:
    fmt.Println(result)  // Output: Task 2 completed
    }
}
```

In this example:

- We have two goroutines, task1 and task2, each sending a message to its respective channel after some delay.
- The select statement waits for either ch1 or ch2 to be ready to receive data. Since task2 takes less time, the program prints "Task 2 completed" first.

Non-blocking Operations with select

You can also use the select statement for non-blocking operations. By including a default case, you can specify what should happen if no channel operations are ready.

Example:

```go
go
Copy
package main

import "fmt"
```

```
func main() {
    ch := make(chan int)

    // Non-blocking receive using select
    select {
    case value := <-ch:
        fmt.Println("Received:", value)
    default:
        fmt.Println("No data available")
    }
}
```

In this example, the select statement checks if there is data available on the channel. If no data is available (i.e., the channel is empty), the default case is executed, and the program prints "No data available".

Summary of the select Statement:

- The select statement allows you to wait on multiple channel operations and execute the first one that is ready.
- It is useful for concurrency control, as it enables you to handle multiple communication channels.
- You can use the default case to make the select non-blocking, and time.After for timeouts.

6.5 Practical Concurrency Example: A Multi-Tasking Program

Now that we've learned about goroutines, channels, and the select statement, let's put everything together in a practical example. In this example, we'll build a simple multi-tasking program that performs three tasks concurrently and handles their completion using channels and the select statement.

Example: Multi-Tasking Program

go
Copy

```go
package main

import (
    "fmt"
    "time"
)

func task1(ch chan string) {
    time.Sleep(2 * time.Second)
    ch <- "Task 1 completed"
}

func task2(ch chan string) {
    time.Sleep(1 * time.Second)
    ch <- "Task 2 completed"
}
```

```go
func task3(ch chan string) {
    time.Sleep(3 * time.Second)
    ch <- "Task 3 completed"
}

func main() {
    ch1 := make(chan string)
    ch2 := make(chan string)
    ch3 := make(chan string)

    go task1(ch1)
    go task2(ch2)
    go task3(ch3)

    // Use select to wait for the first task to complete
    for i := 0; i < 3; i++ {
        select {
        case result := <-ch1:
            fmt.Println(result)
        case result := <-ch2:
            fmt.Println(result)
        case result := <-ch3:
            fmt.Println(result)
        }
    }
}
```

Explanation:

- We have three tasks: task1, task2, and task3. Each task sleeps for a different amount of time and then sends a message through a channel when it is completed.
- We start the tasks as goroutines and wait for their results using the select statement in a loop.
- The select statement blocks until one of the tasks finishes, and we print the result. The program ensures that the tasks are handled concurrently, and it prints the task completion messages as they come in.

Output:

arduino

Copy

Task 2 completed

Task 1 completed

Task 3 completed

In this example, the tasks are completed in the order of their execution time (task 2 first, task 1 second, and task 3 last). The select statement helps manage the concurrent execution and ensures that the main program waits for all tasks to complete.

Summary of the Practical Example:

- We used goroutines to run tasks concurrently.
- Channels allowed us to communicate between goroutines and retrieve results.
- The select statement provided concurrency control, ensuring we could handle the completion of tasks as they finished.

123

Go's concurrency model is straightforward and powerful, allowing you to build efficient, scalable applications with minimal effort. With goroutines, channels, and the select statement, you can handle multiple tasks concurrently while keeping your code clean and easy to understand.

Chapter 7: Working with Files and I/O

7.1 Reading Files in Go

In Go, reading files is a common operation, and the standard library provides powerful tools for working with files. The os and io/ioutil packages are typically used for basic file handling, including reading and writing files.

Opening a File for Reading

To read a file in Go, you first need to open it using the os.Open() function. This function returns a file handle and an error. If the file does not exist or there is another issue opening the file, an error is returned.

Basic Example:

```go
Copy
package main

import (
    "fmt"
    "os"
)

func main() {
    file, err := os.Open("example.txt")  // Open the file for reading
    if err != nil {
        fmt.Println("Error opening file:", err)
```

```
    return
}

defer file.Close() // Ensure the file is closed after the function completes

// Read the contents of the file
fmt.Println("File opened successfully")
}
```

In this example:

- We open the file "example.txt" for reading using os.Open().
- If an error occurs, such as the file not existing, we print the error and exit the program.
- We use defer file.Close() to ensure that the file is closed after the main function finishes executing, even if an error occurs.

Reading the File's Contents

To read the contents of the file, you can use methods like Read(), ReadLine(), or ioutil.ReadFile(), depending on your needs.

1. **Using Read() Method**: The Read() method reads data from the file into a byte slice.

go

Copy

```
package main

import (
```

```go
    "fmt"
    "os"
)

func main() {
    file, err := os.Open("example.txt")
    if err != nil {
        fmt.Println("Error opening file:", err)
        return
    }
    defer file.Close()

    buffer := make([]byte, 100) // Create a buffer to hold the data
    bytesRead, err := file.Read(buffer)
    if err != nil {
        fmt.Println("Error reading file:", err)
        return
    }
    fmt.Printf("Read %d bytes: %s\n", bytesRead, string(buffer[:bytesRead]))
}
```

In this example:

- We create a buffer to hold the data that will be read from the file.
- The file.Read() method reads data from the file into the buffer. It returns the number of bytes read and any error that occurred during the read operation.

127

- We then print the number of bytes read and convert the buffer into a string to display the contents.

2. **Using ioutil.ReadFile()**: If you want to read the entire file at once into memory, you can use ioutil.ReadFile(), which simplifies the reading process.

go

Copy

```go
package main

import (
    "fmt"
    "io/ioutil"
)

func main() {
    data, err := ioutil.ReadFile("example.txt")
    if err != nil {
        fmt.Println("Error reading file:", err)
        return
    }
    fmt.Println("File contents:\n", string(data))
}
```

This example:

- Uses ioutil.ReadFile() to read the entire file into a byte slice (data).
- The contents of the file are printed as a string by converting the byte slice into a string.

128

Handling Errors While Reading Files

Always check for errors when working with files. Files might not exist, or you might not have permission to read them, which would result in an error being returned by os.Open() or ioutil.ReadFile().

Reading a File Line-by-Line

Sometimes you might want to process a file line-by-line instead of reading the whole file at once. You can achieve this by using bufio.Scanner to read the file one line at a time.

```go
go
Copy
package main

import (
    "bufio"
    "fmt"
    "os"
)

func main() {
    file, err := os.Open("example.txt")
    if err != nil {
        fmt.Println("Error opening file:", err)
        return
    }
    defer file.Close()
```

129

```go
scanner := bufio.NewScanner(file)
for scanner.Scan() {
    fmt.Println(scanner.Text())  // Print each line
}

if err := scanner.Err(); err != nil {
    fmt.Println("Error reading file:", err)
}
}
```

In this example:

- We use bufio.NewScanner() to read the file line by line.
- scanner.Scan() reads the next line, and scanner.Text() returns the current line.
- After all lines are read, we check if any errors occurred during the scanning process using scanner.Err().

Summary of Reading Files:

- Use os.Open() to open a file for reading.
- Use Read(), ReadLine(), or ioutil.ReadFile() to read file contents.
- Always check for errors when opening and reading files.
- Use bufio.Scanner for line-by-line reading of a file.

7.2 Writing to Files

Writing to files is just as important as reading files. In Go, writing to a file is done using the os and bufio packages, and the process is fairly straightforward.

Opening a File for Writing

To write to a file in Go, you first need to open the file. The os.OpenFile() function is used to open a file for reading or writing, and it allows you to specify whether to create a new file if it doesn't exist and whether to append to an existing file or overwrite it.

Basic Example of Writing to a File:

```go
Copy
package main

import (
    "fmt"
    "os"
)

func main() {
    file, err := os.OpenFile("example.txt",
os.O_APPEND|os.O_CREATE|os.O_WRONLY, 0644)
    if err != nil {
        fmt.Println("Error opening file:", err)
        return
    }
```

```go
    defer file.Close()

    // Write data to the file
    _, err = file.WriteString("Hello, Go!\n")
    if err != nil {
        fmt.Println("Error writing to file:", err)
        return
    }

    fmt.Println("Data written to file successfully!")
}
```

In this example:

- os.OpenFile() is used to open the file "example.txt" for appending (os.O_APPEND), creating it if it doesn't exist (os.O_CREATE), and allowing write-only access (os.O_WRONLY).
- 0644 specifies the file's permissions (read and write for the owner, read-only for others).
- We use file.WriteString() to write the string "Hello, Go!\n" to the file.
- After writing, we ensure that the file is closed using defer file.Close().

Writing Multiple Lines to a File

To write multiple lines or more complex data, you can use bufio.Writer, which buffers writes to the file and improves performance.

go

132

Copy

```go
package main

import (
    "bufio"
    "fmt"
    "os"
)

func main() {
    file, err := os.OpenFile("example.txt",
os.O_APPEND|os.O_CREATE|os.O_WRONLY, 0644)
    if err != nil {
        fmt.Println("Error opening file:", err)
        return
    }
    defer file.Close()

    writer := bufio.NewWriter(file)
    _, err = writer.WriteString("Writing multiple lines to the file.\n")
    if err != nil {
        fmt.Println("Error writing to file:", err)
        return
    }

    writer.WriteString("Another line of text.\n")
    writer.Flush() // Make sure the data is written to the file
```

```
    fmt.Println("Data written to file successfully!")
}
```

In this example:

- We create a bufio.Writer to buffer the writes to the file, which is more efficient for multiple writes.
- The Flush() method is called to ensure all buffered data is written to the file.

Creating a New File

If you want to create a new file, you can use the os.Create() function. This function creates a new file and opens it for writing. If the file already exists, it will be overwritten.

go
Copy
```
package main

import (
    "fmt"
    "os"
)

func main() {
    file, err := os.Create("newfile.txt")
    if err != nil {
```

```
    fmt.Println("Error creating file:", err)
    return
}
defer file.Close()

// Write data to the new file
_, err = file.WriteString("This is a new file!\n")
if err != nil {
    fmt.Println("Error writing to file:", err)
    return
}

fmt.Println("New file created and data written successfully!")
}
```

In this example:

- os.Create() is used to create a new file, and if the file already exists, it's overwritten.
- The WriteString() method writes text to the newly created file.

Summary of Writing to Files:

- Use os.OpenFile() to open a file for writing and specify the file's creation and access modes.
- Use file.WriteString() to write text to the file.
- Use bufio.Writer for efficient writing of multiple lines to a file.
- Use os.Create() to create a new file and write to it.

Go provides simple yet powerful tools for reading and writing files, which are essential for handling data in real-world applications. With these tools, you can easily manage file I/O operations, handle errors, and ensure that your program interacts with files correctly.

7.3 Handling File Errors and Closing Files

When working with files, it's important to handle errors properly to ensure your program behaves as expected. Errors can arise for various reasons, such as the file not being found, the program lacking proper permissions, or reaching the end of a file. Understanding how to handle file errors is essential for creating reliable applications.

Handling File Errors

In Go, file operations often return an error value to indicate if something went wrong. You should always check for errors after performing file operations to handle potential failures appropriately.

Example of Handling Errors when Opening a File:

```go
Copy
package main

import (
    "fmt"
    "os"
)

func main() {
```

```go
file, err := os.Open("nonexistent.txt")  // Try to open a file that doesn't exist
if err != nil {
    fmt.Println("Error opening file:", err)  // Handle the error if the file is not found
    return
}
defer file.Close()  // Ensure the file is closed after the operation

fmt.Println("File opened successfully")
}
```

In this example:

- The os.Open() function is used to open a file. If the file doesn't exist, an error is returned.
- The error is checked, and if there is an issue opening the file, we print the error and return from the function early.
- If the file opens successfully, the program proceeds, and we ensure the file is closed with defer.

Handling Errors When Writing to a File

Similarly, when writing to a file, always check for errors to ensure the data is written successfully.

go
Copy
```go
package main
```

```go
import (
    "fmt"
    "os"
)

func main() {
    file, err := os.Create("output.txt") // Create a new file for writing
    if err != nil {
        fmt.Println("Error creating file:", err) // Handle error if file can't be created
        return
    }
    defer file.Close() // Ensure the file is closed after the operation

    _, err = file.WriteString("Hello, Go!") // Write data to the file
    if err != nil {
        fmt.Println("Error writing to file:", err) // Handle error if writing fails
        return
    }

    fmt.Println("Data written to file successfully")
}
```

In this example:

- The file is created using os.Create(). If an error occurs (e.g., the program lacks permissions), it is handled by printing the error message and returning from the function.
- When writing to the file using WriteString(), we again check for errors and handle them accordingly.

Closing Files

It's crucial to close files after you're done with them to free up system resources. In Go, you can use the defer statement to ensure that files are closed when the function completes, even if an error occurs.

The defer keyword schedules the Close() method to be called when the surrounding function returns.

Example:

```go
Copy
package main

import (
    "fmt"
    "os"
)

func main() {
    file, err := os.Open("example.txt")
    if err != nil {
```

```
    fmt.Println("Error opening file:", err)
    return
}
defer file.Close() // Ensure the file is closed after the operation

// Perform file operations...
fmt.Println("File opened successfully")
}
```

In this case:

- defer file.Close() ensures that the file is closed after the function completes, even if an error occurs during the file operations.

Summary of Handling File Errors and Closing Files:

- Always check for errors when opening, reading, and writing files.
- Handle errors gracefully, informing the user or taking appropriate action if the operation fails.
- Use defer to close files, ensuring they are closed regardless of whether the function exits successfully or due to an error.

7.4 Working with Directories and File Paths

In addition to reading from and writing to files, working with directories and file paths is essential for managing file systems in Go. Go provides several functions in the os and path/filepath packages for creating, removing, and manipulating directories and file paths.

Working with Directories

Go provides functions for creating, removing, and checking directories. The os package allows you to perform basic directory operations.

1. **Creating Directories**:

You can create a new directory using os.Mkdir() or os.MkdirAll(). The Mkdir() function creates a single directory, while MkdirAll() creates all necessary parent directories as well.

Example:

```go
Copy
package main

import (
    "fmt"
    "os"
)

func main() {
    err := os.Mkdir("newdir", 0755) // Create a directory with permissions
    if err != nil {
        fmt.Println("Error creating directory:", err)
        return
```

141

```
    }
    fmt.Println("Directory created successfully")
}
```

In this example:

- We use os.Mkdir() to create a new directory called "newdir".
- The second argument (0755) sets the directory permissions (read, write, and execute for the owner, and read and execute for others).

2. **Removing Directories**:

You can remove an empty directory using os.Remove(). If the directory is not empty, you can use os.RemoveAll() to delete the directory and its contents.

Example:

go
Copy
```
package main

import (
    "fmt"
    "os"
)

func main() {
    err := os.Remove("newdir") // Remove an empty directory
    if err != nil {
```

142

```go
        fmt.Println("Error removing directory:", err)
        return
    }
    fmt.Println("Directory removed successfully")
}
```

3. Checking if a Directory Exists:

To check if a directory exists, you can use os.Stat() to get information about the directory. If the directory exists, you can check its Mode() to determine if it's a directory.

Example:

go
Copy

```go
package main

import (
    "fmt"
    "os"
)

func main() {
    _, err := os.Stat("newdir")
    if os.IsNotExist(err) {
        fmt.Println("Directory does not exist")
    } else {
        fmt.Println("Directory exists")
```

```
        }
    }
```

Working with File Paths

The path/filepath package provides functions for manipulating file paths in a way that works across different operating systems.

1. Join Paths:

You can use filepath.Join() to join multiple components into a single path. This is cross-platform and takes care of using the correct path separator (/ on Unix-based systems, \ on Windows).

Example:

```go
Copy
package main

import (
    "fmt"
    "path/filepath"
)

func main() {
    path := filepath.Join("folder", "subfolder", "file.txt")
    fmt.Println("Joined path:", path)
}
```
144

2. Get the Base or Directory Name:

You can use filepath.Base() to get the file or directory name from a path, and filepath.Dir() to get the directory of the file.

Example:

go
Copy

```go
package main

import (
    "fmt"
    "path/filepath"
)

func main() {
    path := "/home/user/docs/file.txt"
    fmt.Println("Base:", filepath.Base(path)) // Output: file.txt
    fmt.Println("Directory:", filepath.Dir(path)) // Output: /home/user/docs
}
```

3. Walking through Directories:

You can use filepath.Walk() to recursively walk through all the files and directories within a given directory.

145

Example:

go
Copy
```go
package main

import (
    "fmt"
    "path/filepath"
    "os"
)

func main() {
    err := filepath.Walk("some_directory", func(path string, info os.FileInfo, err error)
error {
        if err != nil {
            fmt.Println("Error walking path:", err)
            return err
        }
        fmt.Println(path)
        return nil
    })
    if err != nil {
        fmt.Println("Error walking the directory:", err)
    }
}
```

Summary of Working with Directories and File Paths:

- Use os.Mkdir() and os.Remove() to create and remove directories.
- Use os.Stat() to check if a directory exists.
- Use filepath.Join(), filepath.Base(), and filepath.Dir() for cross-platform file path manipulation.
- Use filepath.Walk() for recursively walking through directories.

7.5 Practical Example: Building a Simple File Logger

Now that we've covered how to work with files, directories, and file paths, let's build a practical example—a simple file logger. This logger will append log messages to a file with timestamps.

Example: Simple File Logger

go
Copy
```
package main

import (
    "fmt"
    "os"
    "time"
)

func logToFile(filename, message string) {
```

```go
// Open the file for appending
file, err := os.OpenFile(filename, os.O_APPEND|os.O_CREATE|os.O_WRONLY, 0644)
if err != nil {
    fmt.Println("Error opening file:", err)
    return
}
defer file.Close()

// Create a timestamp for the log entry
timestamp := time.Now().Format("2006-01-02 15:04:05")

// Write the log message to the file
logMessage := fmt.Sprintf("%s - %s\n", timestamp, message)
_, err = file.WriteString(logMessage)
if err != nil {
    fmt.Println("Error writing to file:", err)
} else {
    fmt.Println("Log written successfully")
}
}

func main() {
    logToFile("log.txt", "Application started")
    logToFile("log.txt", "Performing some task")
    logToFile("log.txt", "Application ended")
}
```

148

Explanation:

- The logToFile function accepts a filename and a message, opens the file in append mode, and writes the message with a timestamp.
- The time.Now().Format() function is used to format the current time into a readable format.
- The log message is written to the file using file.WriteString().
- The main function logs three different messages to the file "log.txt".

Output (in the log.txt file):

yaml

Copy

2025-01-30 12:00:01 - Application started
2025-01-30 12:00:02 - Performing some task
2025-01-30 12:00:03 - Application ended

Summary of File Logger Example:

- We used os.OpenFile() to open a file in append mode, ensuring that new log messages are added without overwriting the existing content.
- We used time.Now().Format() to add timestamps to each log entry.
- This example demonstrates how to manage file I/O operations, handle errors, and append content to files, all while logging important information.

This simple file logger is a useful tool for tracking application behavior, error reporting, and other logging purposes.

Chapter 8: Web Development with Go

8.1 Introduction to Web Development in Go

Go has become a popular choice for web development due to its simplicity, efficiency, and built-in support for concurrency. It is often praised for its speed and scalability, making it well-suited for building web applications and microservices.

Go's standard library provides powerful tools for handling HTTP requests and responses, making it a great language for building web servers. While Go doesn't have as many high-level frameworks as some other languages, its simplicity and speed allow developers to build fast and efficient web applications.

Some of the advantages of using Go for web development include:

1. **Performance**: Go compiles to machine code, making it fast and efficient. This is especially useful for building high-performance web applications.
2. **Concurrency**: Go's built-in concurrency model (using goroutines and channels) makes it easy to handle many concurrent requests, making it a great choice for building scalable applications.
3. **Standard Library**: Go comes with a powerful standard library that provides everything you need to handle HTTP requests, serve static files, work with databases, and more. You don't need to rely on external frameworks for basic web development tasks.
4. **Simplicity**: Go's syntax is simple and minimalistic, making it easy to learn and use. This is particularly beneficial for small and medium-sized web applications where speed and maintainability are key.

In this chapter, we'll cover how to set up a basic web server in Go, handle HTTP requests, and start building web applications.

Setting Up the Development Environment

Before we dive into web development, ensure that you have Go installed on your system. If not, follow the installation instructions on the official Go website: https://golang.org/doc/install.

Once Go is installed, you can create a new directory for your project and start writing Go code for the web server.

Creating a Simple Web Server

In Go, creating a web server is relatively straightforward. The net/http package in the standard library provides the necessary tools to start an HTTP server, handle requests, and route them to the appropriate handlers.

The most basic web server in Go can be set up in just a few lines of code.

Basic Example of a Web Server in Go:

```go
Copy
package main

import (
    "fmt"
    "net/http"
)
```

```go
// HelloHandler handles requests to the "/hello" path
func HelloHandler(w http.ResponseWriter, r *http.Request) {
    fmt.Fprintln(w, "Hello, Go Web Development!")
}

func main() {
    // Register the HelloHandler function to handle requests to the "/hello" path
    http.HandleFunc("/hello", HelloHandler)

    // Start the web server on port 8080
    fmt.Println("Starting server on :8080...")
    if err := http.ListenAndServe(":8080", nil); err != nil {
        fmt.Println("Error starting server:", err)
    }
}
```

Explanation:

- The http.HandleFunc() function registers a handler function for a specific path (/hello in this case).
- The HelloHandler function is responsible for handling requests to the /hello endpoint. It takes an http.ResponseWriter and an http.Request as arguments, which are used to send the response and read the incoming request, respectively.
- The http.ListenAndServe(":8080", nil) function starts the web server and listens on port 8080. If the server fails to start, an error message is displayed.

Running the Web Server:

1. Save the code in a file named main.go.
2. Open a terminal and navigate to the directory where the file is located.
3. Run the following command:

bash

Copy

```
go run main.go
```

4. You should see the message "Starting server on :8080..." printed in the terminal.
5. Open a web browser and visit http://localhost:8080/hello. You should see the message "Hello, Go Web Development!".

Summary of Web Development in Go:

- Go's net/http package makes it easy to create simple web servers.
- The http.HandleFunc() function registers handlers for specific paths.
- The http.ListenAndServe() function starts the server and listens for incoming HTTP requests.

8.2 Setting Up a Basic Web Server

Now that we have a basic web server running, let's dive deeper into building a more structured web server. In this section, we will explore how to handle different HTTP methods, serve static files, and use URL parameters.

Handling Different HTTP Methods

When building a web application, it's common to handle different HTTP methods like GET, POST, PUT, and DELETE. These methods correspond to different types of actions, such as retrieving data, submitting forms, updating resources, and deleting data.

You can specify which HTTP methods a handler function should respond to by using the http.MethodGet, http.MethodPost, etc., or by handling them in your own custom handler.

Example: Handling Different HTTP Methods:

```go
package main

import (
    "fmt"
    "net/http"
)

func HelloHandler(w http.ResponseWriter, r *http.Request) {
    if r.Method == http.MethodGet {
        fmt.Fprintln(w, "Hello from a GET request!")
    } else if r.Method == http.MethodPost {
        fmt.Fprintln(w, "Hello from a POST request!")
    } else {
        http.Error(w, "Invalid request method", http.StatusMethodNotAllowed)
    }
```

```
}

func main() {
    http.HandleFunc("/hello", HelloHandler)

    fmt.Println("Starting server on :8080...")
    if err := http.ListenAndServe(":8080", nil); err != nil {
        fmt.Println("Error starting server:", err)
    }
}
```

In this example:

- The HelloHandler function checks the HTTP method of the incoming request using r.Method.
- If the method is GET, it responds with "Hello from a GET request!".
- If the method is POST, it responds with "Hello from a POST request!".
- If the method is anything other than GET or POST, the server responds with an error message using http.Error().

Serving Static Files

A common requirement in web development is serving static files such as HTML, CSS, JavaScript, and images. Go makes it easy to serve static files using the http.ServeFile() function or the http.FileServer() handler.

Example: Serving Static Files:

go
Copy
```go
package main

import (
    "fmt"
    "net/http"
)

func main() {
    // Serve files from the "static" directory
    http.Handle("/static/", http.StripPrefix("/static/", http.FileServer(http.Dir("./static"))))

    fmt.Println("Starting server on :8080...")
    if err := http.ListenAndServe(":8080", nil); err != nil {
        fmt.Println("Error starting server:", err)
    }
}
```

In this example:

- The http.Handle() function is used to map the /static/ URL path to the static directory on the file system.

- http.StripPrefix("/static/", http.FileServer(http.Dir("./static"))) serves files from the ./static directory. The StripPrefix function removes the /static/ prefix from the URL so that the remaining path corresponds to the file name in the static folder.

To test this:

1. Create a folder named static in the same directory as your Go file.
2. Place an HTML file (e.g., index.html) inside the static folder.
3. Start the server with go run main.go.
4. Visit http://localhost:8080/static/index.html in your browser to see the static file being served.

Using URL Parameters

Web servers often need to handle dynamic routes with parameters. In Go, you can access URL parameters using the r.URL.Path or use third-party libraries for more advanced routing.

Example: Handling URL Parameters:

go
Copy

```
package main

import (
    "fmt"
    "net/http"
)

func GreetHandler(w http.ResponseWriter, r *http.Request) {
```

```go
    // Extract the name parameter from the URL
    name := r.URL.Path[len("/greet/"):]
    fmt.Fprintf(w, "Hello, %s!", name)
}

func main() {
    http.HandleFunc("/greet/", GreetHandler)

    fmt.Println("Starting server on :8080...")
    if err := http.ListenAndServe(":8080", nil); err != nil {
        fmt.Println("Error starting server:", err)
    }
}
```

In this example:

- The GreetHandler function extracts the name from the URL path. For example, if the URL is /greet/John, the handler extracts "John" and responds with "Hello, John!".
- This method uses basic string manipulation to extract URL parameters. More complex routing can be handled with third-party libraries like gorilla/mux.

Summary of Setting Up a Basic Web Server:

- You can handle different HTTP methods using r.Method.
- Go makes it easy to serve static files using http.FileServer() and http.ServeFile().
- URL parameters can be extracted from the path, allowing you to build dynamic routes.

- The http.HandleFunc() function is the foundation for routing in a basic Go web server.

By building a web server in Go, you can create efficient, scalable, and performant web applications. The Go standard library provides everything you need to handle HTTP requests, serve static content, and create dynamic routes, making it an excellent choice for web development.

8.3 Handling HTTP Requests and Responses

In Go, handling HTTP requests and responses is one of the core aspects of web development. The net/http package provides a simple way to handle HTTP requests, extract data from the request, and craft the appropriate response. Understanding how to handle HTTP requests and responses effectively is crucial for building web applications and services.

Handling HTTP Requests

When an HTTP request is made to your server, Go creates an http.Request object, which contains all the information about the request, such as the HTTP method (GET, POST, etc.), headers, URL, and any data sent in the request body.

You can access data from the http.Request object to process the request, handle query parameters, or extract data from the request body.

Example: Handling GET Request and Query Parameters

go
Copy
package main

```go
import (
    "fmt"
    "net/http"
)

func GreetHandler(w http.ResponseWriter, r *http.Request) {
    // Get the "name" query parameter from the URL
    name := r.URL.Query().Get("name")

    if name == "" {
        name = "Guest"  // Use "Guest" if no name is provided
    }

    // Write a response using the name parameter
    fmt.Fprintf(w, "Hello, %s!", name)
}

func main() {
    // Handle requests to the /greet path
    http.HandleFunc("/greet", GreetHandler)

    fmt.Println("Starting server on :8080...")
    if err := http.ListenAndServe(":8080", nil); err != nil {
        fmt.Println("Error starting server:", err)
    }
}
```

Explanation:

- The GreetHandler function extracts the name query parameter from the URL using r.URL.Query().Get("name").
- If no name is provided, it defaults to "Guest".
- The response is written back to the client using fmt.Fprintf(), which writes the greeting message to the http.ResponseWriter.

Example: Handling POST Request and Request Body

For POST requests, the request body typically contains data (e.g., form data or JSON). You can read this data using r.Body, which returns an io.Reader.

Example:

go
Copy
```go
package main

import (
    "encoding/json"
    "fmt"
    "net/http"
)

type Person struct {
    Name string `json:"name"`
    Age  int    `json:"age"`
```

161

```go
    }

func PersonHandler(w http.ResponseWriter, r *http.Request) {
    if r.Method == http.MethodPost {
        var person Person
        decoder := json.NewDecoder(r.Body)
        if err := decoder.Decode(&person); err != nil {
            http.Error(w, "Invalid request body", http.StatusBadRequest)
            return
        }

        // Respond with the received data
        fmt.Fprintf(w, "Received person: %s, Age: %d", person.Name, person.Age)
    } else {
        http.Error(w, "Invalid HTTP method", http.StatusMethodNotAllowed)
    }
}

func main() {
    http.HandleFunc("/person", PersonHandler)

    fmt.Println("Starting server on :8080...")
    if err := http.ListenAndServe(":8080", nil); err != nil {
        fmt.Println("Error starting server:", err)
    }
}
```

Explanation:

- We define a Person struct to hold the data sent in the POST request as JSON.
- We use json.NewDecoder(r.Body) to decode the incoming JSON data into a Person struct.
- The handler responds by printing the name and age of the person that was received.

Handling HTTP Responses

In Go, you can write responses to the client using the http.ResponseWriter object. You can write text, JSON, HTML, or any other data type, depending on the content type.

Example: Sending JSON Responses

go
Copy
```go
package main

import (
    "encoding/json"
    "fmt"
    "net/http"
)

func JSONHandler(w http.ResponseWriter, r *http.Request) {
    response := map[string]string{"message": "Hello, Go!"}

    // Set the content-type to application/json
```

```go
    w.Header().Set("Content-Type", "application/json")
    w.WriteHeader(http.StatusOK)

    // Send JSON response
    if err := json.NewEncoder(w).Encode(response); err != nil {
        fmt.Println("Error encoding JSON:", err)
        http.Error(w, "Internal server error", http.StatusInternalServerError)
    }
}

func main() {
    http.HandleFunc("/json", JSONHandler)

    fmt.Println("Starting server on :8080...")
    if err := http.ListenAndServe(":8080", nil); err != nil {
        fmt.Println("Error starting server:", err)
    }
}
```

Explanation:

- We define a simple map and set the Content-Type header to "application/json".
- The response is sent using json.NewEncoder(w).Encode(response) to encode the map as JSON and send it to the client.
- The server listens for requests on the /json endpoint and responds with the JSON message.

Summary of Handling HTTP Requests and Responses:

- The http.Request object provides data from the incoming request, including HTTP method, URL parameters, and request body.
- You can handle different HTTP methods (GET, POST, etc.) and extract query parameters or body data as needed.
- The http.ResponseWriter allows you to write responses to the client, including setting headers, writing status codes, and sending data in various formats (JSON, plain text, etc.).

8.4 Creating RESTful APIs

REST (Representational State Transfer) is an architectural style used for designing networked applications. A **RESTful API** is a web service that follows REST principles and allows clients to interact with resources using standard HTTP methods (GET, POST, PUT, DELETE).

In Go, you can create RESTful APIs by setting up HTTP handlers to handle requests, process data, and return appropriate responses. Go's simplicity and powerful standard library make it a great choice for building RESTful APIs.

Principles of RESTful APIs:

- **Stateless**: Each request is independent, and the server doesn't store client session data.
- **Resources**: RESTful APIs focus on resources (data objects), and each resource is identified by a URL.
- **HTTP Methods**: Standard HTTP methods are used to interact with resources:

- ○ GET to retrieve data.
- ○ POST to create new data.
- ○ PUT to update existing data.
- ○ DELETE to remove data.

Creating a Simple RESTful API in Go:

Let's create a simple RESTful API for managing a collection of books. Each book has a title and an author. We will support the following operations:

- GET /books to retrieve the list of books.
- POST /books to add a new book.
- GET /books/{id} to retrieve a specific book.
- DELETE /books/{id} to delete a specific book.

Example:

go
Copy

```go
package main

import (
    "encoding/json"
    "fmt"
    "net/http"
    "strconv"
    "sync"
)
```

```go
type Book struct {
    ID     int    `json:"id"`
    Title  string `json:"title"`
    Author string `json:"author"`
}

var books []Book
var idCounter int
var mu sync.Mutex

func getBooksHandler(w http.ResponseWriter, r *http.Request) {
    mu.Lock()
    defer mu.Unlock()
    w.Header().Set("Content-Type", "application/json")
    w.WriteHeader(http.StatusOK)
    json.NewEncoder(w).Encode(books)
}

func getBookHandler(w http.ResponseWriter, r *http.Request) {
    mu.Lock()
    defer mu.Unlock()

    idStr := r.URL.Path[len("/books/"):]
    id, err := strconv.Atoi(idStr)
    if err != nil || id < 0 || id >= len(books) {
        http.Error(w, "Book not found", http.StatusNotFound)
        return
```

```go
	}

	w.Header().Set("Content-Type", "application/json")
	w.WriteHeader(http.StatusOK)
	json.NewEncoder(w).Encode(books[id])
}

func createBookHandler(w http.ResponseWriter, r *http.Request) {
	mu.Lock()
	defer mu.Unlock()

	var book Book
	if err := json.NewDecoder(r.Body).Decode(&book); err != nil {
		http.Error(w, "Invalid request body", http.StatusBadRequest)
		return
	}

	idCounter++
	book.ID = idCounter
	books = append(books, book)

	w.Header().Set("Content-Type", "application/json")
	w.WriteHeader(http.StatusCreated)
	json.NewEncoder(w).Encode(book)
}

func deleteBookHandler(w http.ResponseWriter, r *http.Request) {
```

```go
    mu.Lock()
    defer mu.Unlock()

    idStr := r.URL.Path[len("/books/"):]
    id, err := strconv.Atoi(idStr)
    if err != nil || id < 0 || id >= len(books) {
        http.Error(w, "Book not found", http.StatusNotFound)
        return
    }

    books = append(books[:id], books[id+1:]...)

    w.WriteHeader(http.StatusNoContent)
}

func main() {
    // Initial book data
    books = []Book{
        {ID: 1, Title: "Go Programming", Author: "John Doe"},
        {ID: 2, Title: "Learn Go", Author: "Jane Smith"},
    }

    http.HandleFunc("/books", getBooksHandler)        // GET /books
    http.HandleFunc("/books/", getBookHandler)        // GET /books/{id}
    http.HandleFunc("/books", createBookHandler)      // POST /books
    http.HandleFunc("/books/", deleteBookHandler)     // DELETE /books/{id}
```

```
fmt.Println("Starting server on :8080...")
if err := http.ListenAndServe(":8080", nil); err != nil {
    fmt.Println("Error starting server:", err)
}
}
```

Explanation:

- The Book struct represents a book with an ID, Title, and Author.
- We use a global books slice to store the list of books and a mutex (mu) to prevent race conditions when modifying the slice.
- Each handler function corresponds to one of the RESTful operations:
  - getBooksHandler: Returns the list of books (GET /books).
  - getBookHandler: Returns a single book based on its ID (GET /books/{id}).
  - createBookHandler: Adds a new book to the list (POST /books).
  - deleteBookHandler: Deletes a book by its ID (DELETE /books/{id}).

Summary of Creating RESTful APIs:

- RESTful APIs use standard HTTP methods (GET, POST, PUT, DELETE) to interact with resources.
- In Go, you can create RESTful APIs by handling requests with http.HandleFunc() and writing JSON responses with json.NewEncoder().
- Go's simplicity and concurrency model make it an excellent choice for building fast and scalable web APIs.

8.5 Practical Example: Building a Simple Web API

Let's put everything together and create a simple web API. In this example, we'll build a basic API that allows you to manage a collection of books. This API will include endpoints to view all books, view a single book, create a new book, and delete a book.

Example: Simple Web API for Managing Books

go
Copy

```go
package main

import (
    "encoding/json"
    "fmt"
    "net/http"
    "strconv"
    "sync"
)

type Book struct {
    ID     int    `json:"id"`
    Title  string `json:"title"`
    Author string `json:"author"`
}

var books []Book
var idCounter int
```

```go
var mu sync.Mutex

func getBooksHandler(w http.ResponseWriter, r *http.Request) {
    mu.Lock()
    defer mu.Unlock()

    w.Header().Set("Content-Type", "application/json")
    w.WriteHeader(http.StatusOK)
    json.NewEncoder(w).Encode(books)
}

func getBookHandler(w http.ResponseWriter, r *http.Request) {
    mu.Lock()
    defer mu.Unlock()

    idStr := r.URL.Path[len("/books/"):]
    id, err := strconv.Atoi(idStr)
    if err != nil || id < 0 || id >= len(books) {
        http.Error(w, "Book not found", http.StatusNotFound)
        return
    }

    w.Header().Set("Content-Type", "application/json")
    w.WriteHeader(http.StatusOK)
    json.NewEncoder(w).Encode(books[id])
}
```

```go
func createBookHandler(w http.ResponseWriter, r *http.Request) {
    mu.Lock()
    defer mu.Unlock()

    var book Book
    if err := json.NewDecoder(r.Body).Decode(&book); err != nil {
        http.Error(w, "Invalid request body", http.StatusBadRequest)
        return
    }

    idCounter++
    book.ID = idCounter
    books = append(books, book)

    w.Header().Set("Content-Type", "application/json")
    w.WriteHeader(http.StatusCreated)
    json.NewEncoder(w).Encode(book)
}

func deleteBookHandler(w http.ResponseWriter, r *http.Request) {
    mu.Lock()
    defer mu.Unlock()

    idStr := r.URL.Path[len("/books/"):]
    id, err := strconv.Atoi(idStr)
    if err != nil || id < 0 || id >= len(books) {
        http.Error(w, "Book not found", http.StatusNotFound)
```

```go
        return
    }

    books = append(books[:id], books[id+1:]...)

    w.WriteHeader(http.StatusNoContent)
}

func main() {
    // Initial book data
    books = []Book{
        {ID: 1, Title: "Go Programming", Author: "John Doe"},
        {ID: 2, Title: "Learn Go", Author: "Jane Smith"},
    }

    http.HandleFunc("/books", getBooksHandler)      // GET /books
    http.HandleFunc("/books/", getBookHandler)      // GET /books/{id}
    http.HandleFunc("/books", createBookHandler)    // POST /books
    http.HandleFunc("/books/", deleteBookHandler)   // DELETE /books/{id}

    fmt.Println("Starting server on :8080...")
    if err := http.ListenAndServe(":8080", nil); err != nil {
        fmt.Println("Error starting server:", err)
    }
}
```

174

In this example, we've built a simple RESTful API for managing books. The API has four endpoints:

1. GET /books: Returns a list of all books.
2. GET /books/{id}: Returns a specific book based on its ID.
3. POST /books: Creates a new book by accepting a JSON payload.
4. DELETE /books/{id}: Deletes a book by its ID.

To test this API:

1. Run the Go application.
2. Use a tool like Postman or curl to make requests to the API.

Summary of Practical Example:

- We created a simple RESTful API for managing books.
- We handled different HTTP methods (GET, POST, DELETE) to interact with the books resource.
- We used json.NewEncoder() to send JSON responses and handle JSON request bodies.
- This example demonstrates how to build a basic, functional web API in Go.

Chapter 9: Go Standard Library and Useful Packages

9.1 Overview of Go's Standard Library

Go's standard library is one of its most compelling features. It includes a vast collection of packages that provide essential functionality for a wide range of programming tasks, from working with files and directories to handling HTTP requests, processing text, performing mathematical operations, and more. The Go standard library is designed to be simple, well-documented, and efficient, allowing developers to write powerful applications with minimal dependencies.

Key Features of Go's Standard Library:

1. **Comprehensive**: The standard library includes packages for networking, web development, cryptography, text manipulation, file I/O, concurrency, and more.
2. **Ease of Use**: Go's standard library is designed with simplicity in mind, making it easy for developers to perform common tasks without needing third-party libraries.
3. **Performance**: The packages in the standard library are highly optimized for performance, ensuring that Go programs are both fast and efficient.
4. **Cross-Platform**: Go's standard library is cross-platform, meaning that code written using these packages will work across different operating systems without modification.

In this chapter, we'll dive into some of the most commonly used packages in Go's standard library, including fmt, strings, and math. These packages are essential for a wide range of tasks, from formatting output and working with strings to performing mathematical calculations.

9.2 Using the fmt, strings, and math Packages

Let's explore the fmt, strings, and math packages, which are among the most frequently used packages in Go.

fmt Package

The fmt package provides formatted I/O functions that allow you to print output to the console, format strings, and read input from the user. It is one of the core packages in Go for performing input and output operations.

Common Functions in the fmt Package:

- fmt.Print(): Prints output to the console without a newline.
- fmt.Println(): Prints output to the console with a newline at the end.
- fmt.Printf(): Prints formatted output, allowing you to control the appearance of the output using format specifiers.
- fmt.Scan(): Reads input from the user.

Example:

go
Copy
package main

```go
import "fmt"

func main() {
    // Print a message without a newline
    fmt.Print("Hello, ")

    // Print a message with a newline
    fmt.Println("Go!")

    // Format a string and print it
    name := "Alice"
    age := 25
    fmt.Printf("%s is %d years old.\n", name, age)
}
```

Explanation:

- fmt.Print() prints "Hello, " without a newline.
- fmt.Println() prints "Go!" with a newline.
- fmt.Printf() formats the string to insert values into the placeholders (%s for a string and %d for an integer) and prints the formatted output.

Format Specifiers:

- %s: For strings.
- %d: For integers (decimal).
- %f: For floating-point numbers.
- %v: For printing a value in its default format.

178

- %t: For booleans.

strings Package

The strings package provides functions for manipulating and processing strings. It contains many useful methods for tasks such as searching, replacing, trimming, and splitting strings.

Common Functions in the strings Package:

- strings.Contains(): Checks if a substring exists within a string.
- strings.ToUpper(): Converts a string to uppercase.
- strings.ToLower(): Converts a string to lowercase.
- strings.TrimSpace(): Removes leading and trailing spaces from a string.
- strings.Split(): Splits a string into a slice of substrings.

Example:

```go
Copy
package main

import (
    "fmt"
    "strings"
)

func main() {
    str := "Hello, Go World!"
```

```go
// Check if the string contains a substring
fmt.Println(strings.Contains(str, "Go")) // Output: true

// Convert the string to uppercase
fmt.Println(strings.ToUpper(str)) // Output: HELLO, GO WORLD!

// Convert the string to lowercase
fmt.Println(strings.ToLower(str)) // Output: hello, go world!

// Trim spaces from the string
strWithSpaces := "  Go Programming  "
fmt.Println(strings.TrimSpace(strWithSpaces)) // Output: Go Programming

// Split the string into substrings
words := strings.Split(str, " ")
fmt.Println(words) // Output: [Hello, Go World!]
}
```

Explanation:

- strings.Contains() checks if the substring "Go" is present in the string "Hello, Go World!".

- strings.ToUpper() and strings.ToLower() convert the string to uppercase and lowercase, respectively.

- strings.TrimSpace() removes any leading or trailing spaces from the string.

- strings.Split() splits the string into substrings by a specified separator (in this case, the space " ").

math **Package**

The math package provides basic mathematical functions for performing calculations like rounding, absolute value, trigonometry, square roots, and more. It is a core package for performing numerical operations in Go.

Common Functions in the math **Package:**

- math.Abs(): Returns the absolute value of a number.
- math.Pow(): Returns the result of raising a number to a power.
- math.Sqrt(): Returns the square root of a number.
- math.Sin(), math.Cos(), math.Tan(): Trigonometric functions for sine, cosine, and tangent.

Example:

go
Copy

```
package main

import (
    "fmt"
    "math"
)

func main() {
```

```
// Calculate the absolute value
fmt.Println(math.Abs(-42.7)) // Output: 42.7

// Calculate the power of a number
fmt.Println(math.Pow(2, 3))  // Output: 8

// Calculate the square root
fmt.Println(math.Sqrt(16))   // Output: 4

// Trigonometric functions (sin, cos, tan)
angle := math.Pi / 4  // 45 degrees in radians
fmt.Println(math.Sin(angle)) // Output: 0.7071067811865475
fmt.Println(math.Cos(angle)) // Output: 0.7071067811865475
fmt.Println(math.Tan(angle)) // Output: 1
}
```

Explanation:

- math.Abs() returns the absolute value of -42.7.
- math.Pow(2, 3) computes 2 raised to the power of 3, resulting in 8.
- math.Sqrt(16) returns the square root of 16, which is 4.
- The trigonometric functions math.Sin(), math.Cos(), and math.Tan() compute the sine, cosine, and tangent of an angle (in radians). In this case, we use math.Pi / 4 to represent 45 degrees.

Summary of fmt, strings, and math Packages:

- The fmt package is used for formatted I/O operations, including printing output and reading input.
- The strings package provides a wide variety of functions for working with strings, including searching, replacing, and splitting strings.
- The math package contains a variety of functions for mathematical operations such as absolute value, powers, square roots, and trigonometry.

Go's standard library offers a rich set of packages that help developers handle many tasks without relying on third-party libraries. The fmt, strings, and math packages are just the beginning. These packages simplify common operations and make Go an ideal choice for building efficient, high-performance applications. With a solid understanding of these packages, you'll be able to solve many problems in a Go application, from handling I/O to performing complex string manipulations and mathematical calculations.

9.3 Working with Time and Dates in Go

Working with time and dates is a crucial part of many applications. In Go, the time package provides a comprehensive set of functions for handling time, such as getting the current time, formatting dates, and performing time calculations. Understanding how to use the time package effectively can help you manage timestamps, durations, and intervals in your applications.

Getting the Current Time

The time.Now() function returns the current local time. It returns a time.Time object, which provides many methods for manipulating and displaying time.

Example:

go

Copy

```go
package main

import (
    "fmt"
    "time"
)

func main() {
    currentTime := time.Now()
    fmt.Println("Current time:", currentTime)
}
```

184

Explanation:

- time.Now() retrieves the current time and prints it in the default format.

Formatting Time and Dates

Go uses a specific reference time to format and parse times: Mon Jan 2 15:04:05 MST 2006. This reference time is used as a pattern for formatting and parsing time, where each component represents a part of the time (e.g., the year, month, day, etc.).

Example:

go

Copy

```go
package main

import (
    "fmt"
    "time"
)
func main() {
    currentTime := time.Now()
```

185

```go
    // Format the current time
    formattedTime := currentTime.Format("2006-01-02 15:04:05")
    fmt.Println("Formatted time:", formattedTime)
}
```

Explanation:

- We use the Format() method to format the current time according to the reference time.
- The format string 2006-01-02 15:04:05 corresponds to the year, month, day, hour, minute, and second.

Parsing Time

You can also parse a string into a time.Time object using the time.Parse() function. You need to provide the format that the date string is in.

Example:

go

Copy

```go
package main

import (
    "fmt"
```

```go
    "time"
)

func main() {
    dateStr := "2025-01-30 14:45:00"

    layout := "2006-01-02 15:04:05"

    parsedTime, err := time.Parse(layout, dateStr)

    if err != nil {

        fmt.Println("Error parsing time:", err)

        return

    }

    fmt.Println("Parsed time:", parsedTime)

}
```

Explanation:

- time.Parse() parses the string "2025-01-30 14:45:00" into a time.Time object.
- We specify the format using the reference time "2006-01-02 15:04:05".

Time Durations

You can work with durations using the time.Duration type, which represents the difference between two times. The Duration type is an integer representing nanoseconds.

187

Example:

go

Copy

```go
package main

import (
    "fmt"
    "time"
)

func main() {
    // Create a duration of 2 hours
    duration := 2 * time.Hour
    fmt.Println("Duration:", duration)

    // Add duration to current time
    currentTime := time.Now()
```

```go
    newTime := currentTime.Add(duration)

    fmt.Println("New time:", newTime)

}
```

Explanation:

- 2 * time.Hour creates a Duration of 2 hours.
- currentTime.Add(duration) adds the 2-hour duration to the current time and prints the result.

Calculating Differences Between Times

You can calculate the difference between two time.Time objects using the Sub() method, which returns a time.Duration.

Example:

go

Copy

```go
package main

import (

    "fmt"

    "time"
```

```
)

func main() {

    time1 := time.Now()

    time2 := time1.Add(3 * time.Hour)


    // Calculate the difference between the two times

    duration := time2.Sub(time1)

    fmt.Println("Time difference:", duration)

}
```

Explanation:

- time2.Sub(time1) calculates the difference between time2 and time1, returning the result as a time.Duration.

Summary of Working with Time and Dates:

- Use time.Now() to get the current local time.
- Use Format() to format time according to a custom layout.
- Use Parse() to convert a string into a time.Time object.
- time.Duration allows you to represent and manipulate time intervals.
- Use Sub() to calculate the difference between two times.

9.4 Essential Go Libraries for Beginners

While the Go standard library provides a lot of functionality, many developers use third-party libraries to enhance their applications. However, for beginners, it's important to focus on a few essential libraries that make Go development more efficient and productive. Here are some key libraries every Go developer should be aware of:

gorilla/mux: A powerful HTTP router and URL matcher for Go. It allows you to define more advanced routes than the basic http.HandleFunc(). It's essential for building complex web applications and APIs.

Example:

go

Copy

```
import "github.com/gorilla/mux"
```

1. gorilla/mux allows you to handle dynamic URL parameters, HTTP methods, and route matching with great flexibility.

logrus: A structured logger for Go, widely used for logging in production environments. It supports different log levels (e.g., info, debug, error) and outputs logs in various formats like JSON.

Example:

go

Copy

```
import "github.com/sirupsen/logrus"
```

2. golang.org/x/net/context: This package provides the Context type, which is essential for managing cancellations, timeouts, and deadlines in concurrent Go

programs. It is often used in web servers and client libraries to manage request lifetimes.

gin-gonic/gin: A fast and flexible HTTP web framework. It's perfect for building APIs and web apps quickly while keeping things lightweight. It offers routing, middleware support, and more.

Example:

go

Copy

```
import "github.com/gin-gonic/gin"
```

3. go-redis/redis: A Redis client for Go, which allows you to interact with Redis databases. It's a great choice if you need to integrate caching or messaging queues into your Go application.

gopkg.in/yaml.v2: A YAML parser and emitter for Go. If you're working with configuration files or other data that uses YAML, this package is a great choice.

Example:

go

Copy

```
import "gopkg.in/yaml.v2"
```

4. jmoiron/sqlx: An extension of the database/sql package that provides additional features like easier SQL querying and support for struct-to-sql mapping. This library simplifies working with databases in Go.

5. testing: The testing package is built into Go's standard library, but it's crucial to mention because it allows for unit testing. Go encourages writing tests as you build your application, and the testing package makes it easy to write and run tests.

6. **go-chi/chi**: A lightweight and idiomatic router for Go. It's similar to gorilla/mux but is even simpler to use for routing and building small, fast web applications.

Summary of Essential Libraries:

- **gorilla/mux**: Advanced HTTP router for building APIs and web apps.
- **logrus**: Structured logger for better logging in Go applications.
- **gin**: A fast and flexible web framework for building APIs and apps.
- **go-redis/redis**: Redis client for Go.
- **gopkg.in/yaml.v2**: YAML parser for configuration files.
- **sqlx**: A database library for simplifying SQL operations in Go.

9.5 Introduction to Third-Party Go Packages

One of Go's strengths is its vibrant ecosystem of third-party libraries and packages. These libraries help developers tackle specific tasks that go beyond what's available in the Go standard library. The Go community has built and maintained a wide array of open-source packages for everything from web development and database interaction to machine learning and data processing.

To use third-party packages in Go, you typically import them into your project using their respective import paths (e.g., "github.com/gorilla/mux"), and you can install them using go get.

How to Install Third-Party Packages:

1. Find the package on pkg.go.dev or GitHub.

Use the go get command to install the package. For example:

bash

Copy

```
go get github.com/gorilla/mux
```

2. Import the package into your Go code:

go

Copy

```
import "github.com/gorilla/mux"
```

3. Once installed, you can use the functionality provided by the package in your code.

Example of Using a Third-Party Package:

go

Copy

```
package main

import (

    "fmt"

    "github.com/gorilla/mux"

    "net/http"
```

194

```
)


func main() {

  r := mux.NewRouter()

  r.HandleFunc("/", func(w http.ResponseWriter, r *http.Request) {

    fmt.Fprintf(w, "Hello, world!")

  })



  http.ListenAndServe(":8080", r)

}
```

In this example:

- We used gorilla/mux to create a router and define a route that handles requests to the root path.
- The mux.NewRouter() creates a new router, and r.HandleFunc() defines the handler for the root route.
- The server starts on port 8080.

Summary of Third-Party Packages:

- Third-party Go packages extend the functionality of the standard library, allowing you to tackle specific tasks more easily.
- You can install third-party packages using go get and import them into your code.
- Popular packages like gorilla/mux (for routing) and gin (for web development) simplify building web applications and APIs.

Go's ecosystem of third-party packages makes it easy to find tools that solve your specific problems and integrate them into your project. Whether you're working on a web app, interacting with a database, or processing data, there's likely a package that can help.

Chapter 10: Object-Oriented Concepts in Go

10.1 Go and Object-Oriented Programming (OOP)

Unlike many other programming languages, Go does not support traditional object-oriented programming (OOP) in the same way that languages like Java or C++ do. Go does not have classes, inheritance, or explicit support for polymorphism, which are all core concepts in traditional OOP. However, Go does provide mechanisms that allow you to achieve many OOP principles such as encapsulation, composition, and abstraction, though they work differently than in other languages.

While Go's approach is more minimalist, it can still be used to build robust and scalable applications. Let's look at how Go approaches the key aspects of OOP:

Key OOP Concepts in Go:

1. **Encapsulation**: In Go, encapsulation is achieved using **structs** and **methods**. You define a struct to represent your object's data, and you associate methods with structs to define the behaviors or actions associated with that object. Go uses **exported** and **unexported** fields and methods to control visibility (similar to private and public access modifiers in other languages).

2. **Composition**: Go does not support inheritance, but it promotes **composition** as a way to combine simple types into more complex ones. A struct can embed other structs, effectively "composing" an object with functionality from multiple types.

3. **Abstraction**: In Go, abstraction is achieved through **interfaces**. Go uses interfaces to define behaviors and allow types to implement them. If a type has methods that match an interface, it implicitly implements that interface, which supports polymorphism without the need for explicit declarations.

Go's Approach to OOP vs. Traditional OOP:

- Go **does not have classes**. Instead, it uses **structs** to represent data and **methods** to define behaviors.
- **No inheritance**. Go supports composition, where structs can embed other structs to reuse functionality.
- **Interfaces** in Go enable polymorphism but without the inheritance-based mechanism seen in traditional OOP.

Despite these differences, Go's minimalistic approach to OOP allows developers to write clean, maintainable, and modular code. You can achieve many OOP principles without the complexity that comes with traditional OOP languages.

10.2 Structs as Objects

In Go, **structs** are the primary mechanism for representing data that can be manipulated. While Go does not have the concept of classes like traditional OOP languages, structs can be thought of as the "object" in Go. A struct can hold fields (data) and methods (behavior), and when combined, they allow you to model objects in your application.

Go allows you to associate methods with structs, and these methods define behaviors that operate on the data within the struct. This allows you to encapsulate related data and behaviors in a cohesive way.

Defining and Using Structs

A **struct** in Go is a composite data type that groups together variables (fields) under one name. Each field can be of a different type. You can define a struct using the type keyword followed by the struct name and its fields.

Example: Defining a Struct

go
Copy

```
package main

import "fmt"

// Define a struct to represent a "Person"
type Person struct {
    FirstName string
    LastName  string
    Age       int
}

func main() {
    // Create an instance of the Person struct
    person := Person{FirstName: "John", LastName: "Doe", Age: 30}

    // Access fields of the struct
    fmt.Println(person.FirstName, person.LastName, person.Age)
}
```

Explanation:

- We define a Person struct with three fields: FirstName, LastName, and Age.
- In the main function, we create an instance of the Person struct and initialize its fields using named values.
- The struct fields can be accessed using the dot (.) notation, like person.FirstName.

Methods on Structs

Go allows you to define **methods** on structs. A method is a function with a special receiver argument that indicates which type the method operates on. This allows you to attach behavior to structs and treat them as objects with both data and behavior.

Example: Defining Methods for Structs

go
Copy

```go
package main

import "fmt"

// Define a struct to represent a "Person"
type Person struct {
    FirstName string
    LastName  string
    Age       int
```

200

```go
}

// Define a method for the Person struct
func (p Person) FullName() string {
    return p.FirstName + " " + p.LastName
}

// Define a method to update the person's age
func (p *Person) HaveBirthday() {
    p.Age++
}

func main() {
    // Create an instance of the Person struct
    person := Person{FirstName: "John", LastName: "Doe", Age: 30}

    // Call methods on the struct
    fmt.Println("Full Name:", person.FullName()) // Output: Full Name: John Doe

    // Call HaveBirthday method to increment the person's age
    person.HaveBirthday()
    fmt.Println("New Age:", person.Age) // Output: New Age: 31
}
```

Explanation:

- The FullName method is a **value method**, which means it operates on a copy of the struct. It does not modify the struct itself.
- The HaveBirthday method is a **pointer method**, meaning it operates on a pointer to the struct. This allows it to modify the struct's fields, such as incrementing the Age field.
- We call these methods using the dot notation on an instance of the struct.

Methods and Pointer Receivers

In Go, you can define methods with **value receivers** or **pointer receivers**.

Value receivers: Methods that operate on copies of the struct. These methods cannot modify the struct.

Example:

go

Copy

```go
func (p Person) FullName() string { ... }
```

1. **Pointer receivers**: Methods that operate on pointers to the struct. These methods can modify the struct's fields.

   Example:

   go

   Copy

   ```go
   func (p *Person) HaveBirthday() { ... }
   ```

2. Composition of Structs (Embedding)

While Go does not have inheritance, it supports **composition** through **embedding**. A struct can embed another struct, which effectively gives it the fields and methods of the embedded struct.

Example: Struct Composition

go
Copy

```
package main

import "fmt"

// Define a struct to represent an Address
type Address struct {
    Street, City, State, Zip string
}

// Define a struct to represent a "Person"
type Person struct {
    FirstName, LastName string
    Age            int
    Address        // Embed Address struct within Person
}

func main() {
    // Create an instance of the Person struct with embedded Address
```

203

```go
    person := Person{
        FirstName: "John",
        LastName:  "Doe",
        Age:       30,
        Address: Address{
            Street: "123 Main St",
            City:   "Somewhere",
            State:  "CA",
            Zip:    "12345",
        },
    }

    // Access both the Person and Address fields
    fmt.Println(person.FirstName, person.LastName, person.Age)
    fmt.Println(person.Address.Street, person.Address.City, person.Address.Zip)
}
```

Explanation:

- The Person struct embeds the Address struct, which allows Person to access the fields of Address directly.
- This is a form of composition, where the Person struct "has" an Address and can access its fields like person.Address.Street.
- Go does not have inheritance, but struct composition allows you to reuse and combine functionality from multiple structs.

Interfaces in Go

Interfaces in Go are another important concept for achieving object-oriented design. An interface is a type that specifies a set of methods. A type implements an interface by providing implementations for those methods. Go uses **implicit interface implementation**, meaning a type does not need to declare that it implements an interface—if the methods match, the type implements the interface.

Example: Interfaces in Go

go
Copy

```
package main

import "fmt"

// Define an interface for shapes
type Shape interface {
    Area() float64
}

// Define a struct for a rectangle
type Rectangle struct {
    Width, Height float64
}

// Implement the Area method for the Rectangle type
func (r Rectangle) Area() float64 {
```

```go
        return r.Width * r.Height
}

// Define a struct for a circle
type Circle struct {
    Radius float64
}

// Implement the Area method for the Circle type
func (c Circle) Area() float64 {
    return 3.14 * c.Radius * c.Radius
}

func printArea(s Shape) {
    fmt.Println("Area:", s.Area())
}

func main() {
    rect := Rectangle{Width: 10, Height: 5}
    circle := Circle{Radius: 7}

    printArea(rect)   // Output: Area: 50
    printArea(circle) // Output: Area: 153.94
}
```

Explanation:

- We define a Shape interface with an Area() method.
- Both Rectangle and Circle structs implement the Area() method, making them types that satisfy the Shape interface.
- The printArea function accepts any type that implements the Shape interface, demonstrating polymorphism.

Summary of Structs as Objects

- **Structs** in Go serve as the primary mechanism for representing objects, encapsulating data and behavior.
- **Methods** can be defined on structs to provide behavior and functionality.
- Go supports **composition** (embedding structs) to combine data and functionality.
- Go uses **interfaces** for polymorphism, allowing types to be used interchangeably if they implement the same set of methods.

In conclusion, while Go doesn't have traditional object-oriented features like classes and inheritance, it provides powerful tools through structs, methods, composition, and interfaces to achieve object-oriented principles in a simpler and more efficient way. This approach allows Go developers to build maintainable, modular, and scalable applications without the complexity found in traditional OOP languages.

10.3 Methods: Associating Functions with Structs

In Go, methods are functions that are associated with a specific type, usually a struct. This is how you add behavior to your structs and essentially mimic object-oriented programming (OOP) behavior. Methods in Go allow you to operate on instances of a type (usually a struct), and they can either modify the instance or return a result based on its data.

A method is defined just like a regular function, but it has an extra receiver argument. This receiver is the type that the method is associated with, and it can either be a value or a pointer.

Value Receivers vs Pointer Receivers

Value receivers: The method works on a copy of the struct, and it does not modify the original instance.
Example:

go

Copy

```go
func (p Person) GetFullName() string {
    return p.FirstName + " " + p.LastName
}
```

1. **Pointer receivers**: The method operates on a reference to the struct, so any changes made to the struct inside the method will affect the original instance.
   Example:

   go

   Copy

   ```go
   func (p *Person) HaveBirthday() {

   p.Age++
   }
   ```

Example: Defining Methods on Structs

go

Copy

```go
package main

import "fmt"

// Define a struct to represent a "Person"
type Person struct {
    FirstName, LastName string
    Age                 int
}

// Method with value receiver: does not modify the struct
func (p Person) FullName() string {
    return p.FirstName + " " + p.LastName
}

// Method with pointer receiver: modifies the struct
func (p *Person) HaveBirthday() {
    p.Age++
}

func main() {
    person := Person{FirstName: "John", LastName: "Doe", Age: 30}

    // Call the FullName method
    fmt.Println(person.FullName())  // Output: John Doe
```

```
// Call the HaveBirthday method
person.HaveBirthday()
fmt.Println(person.Age)  // Output: 31
}
```

Explanation:

- The FullName method uses a **value receiver**, so it does not modify the original person struct.
- The HaveBirthday method uses a **pointer receiver**, so it can modify the person struct (in this case, increasing the Age).

Why Use Methods with Receivers?

- **Value receivers** are suitable when the method does not need to modify the receiver, and it's often more efficient for small structs because no pointer indirection is needed.
- **Pointer receivers** are used when the method needs to modify the struct or when the struct is large, and copying it would be inefficient.

Summary of Methods:

- Methods in Go allow you to associate functions with structs and other types.
- Methods can have value receivers (if they do not modify the struct) or pointer receivers (if they modify the struct).
- This allows you to encapsulate behaviors and operations within structs, which is the core idea behind OOP.

10.4 Interfaces: Defining Behavior in Go

An **interface** in Go is a type that defines a set of method signatures. If a type provides implementations for all the methods in an interface, it **implicitly** satisfies the interface. There is no need to explicitly declare that a type implements an interface, which makes Go's interface system flexible and easy to use.

What is an Interface?

In Go, an interface specifies a set of methods that a type must implement. The type itself does not need to declare that it implements an interface, and an interface does not specify how the methods are implemented. It only describes what methods are available.

Syntax for an Interface:

go
Copy

```go
type InterfaceName interface {
    Method1()
    Method2() string
    // More methods...
}
```

Example: Using Interfaces in Go

go
Copy

```go
package main

import "fmt"
```

```go
// Define a Shape interface with an Area method
type Shape interface {
    Area() float64
}

// Define a Rectangle struct
type Rectangle struct {
    Width, Height float64
}

// Define a Circle struct
type Circle struct {
    Radius float64
}

// Implement the Area method for Rectangle
func (r Rectangle) Area() float64 {
    return r.Width * r.Height
}

// Implement the Area method for Circle
func (c Circle) Area() float64 {
    return 3.14 * c.Radius * c.Radius
}

// Function to print the area of any Shape
```

```go
func printArea(s Shape) {
    fmt.Println("Area:", s.Area())
}

func main() {
    rect := Rectangle{Width: 10, Height: 5}
    circle := Circle{Radius: 7}

    printArea(rect)   // Output: Area: 50
    printArea(circle) // Output: Area: 153.94
}
```

Explanation:

- We define an interface called Shape, which requires an Area() method.
- Both the Rectangle and Circle structs implement the Area() method, so they implicitly satisfy the Shape interface.
- The printArea function accepts any type that implements the Shape interface, demonstrating polymorphism in Go.

Empty Interfaces

The empty interface interface{} is a special case in Go. It is a type that can hold any value, meaning it is a "catch-all" interface. It is similar to Object in other languages.

Example: Using the Empty Interface

go
Copy
```go
package main

import "fmt"

func printAnything(value interface{}) {
    fmt.Println(value)
}

func main() {
    printAnything(42)           // Prints: 42
    printAnything("Hello, Go!") // Prints: Hello, Go!
    printAnything(3.14)         // Prints: 3.14
}
```

Explanation:

- The interface{} type can accept any value (integer, string, float, etc.).
- It allows you to create functions or data structures that work with any type of value.

Type Assertions

A **type assertion** allows you to retrieve the underlying value of an interface. You can use it to assert that an interface contains a specific type and then extract the value.

Example:

go
Copy
```go
package main

import "fmt"

func printString(value interface{}) {
    str, ok := value.(string) // Type assertion
    if ok {
        fmt.Println(str)
    } else {
        fmt.Println("Not a string")
    }
}

func main() {
    printString("Hello, Go!")  // Output: Hello, Go!
    printString(42)            // Output: Not a string
}
```

Explanation:

- value.(string) asserts that the interface value contains a string. If it does, it extracts the string; otherwise, it returns false.

215

Summary of Interfaces:

- Interfaces define a set of methods that a type must implement.
- A type implements an interface implicitly if it provides the required methods.
- The empty interface (interface{}) can hold values of any type.
- Type assertions allow you to extract values from interfaces when you know the underlying type.

10.5 Practical Example: Creating a Simple Go Application Using OOP Principles

Let's apply the object-oriented principles we've discussed to build a simple Go application. In this example, we'll create a program that models a **Vehicle** system with different types of vehicles (e.g., Car, Truck), using Go's struct, methods, and interfaces.

Example: Vehicle System Using OOP Principles

go
Copy

```go
package main

import "fmt"

// Define an interface for vehicles
type Vehicle interface {
    Start() string
    Stop() string
```

```go
}

// Define a struct for Car
type Car struct {
    Make, Model string
}

// Define a struct for Truck
type Truck struct {
    Make, Model string
    Payload     int
}

// Implement the Start method for Car
func (c Car) Start() string {
    return fmt.Sprintf("%s %s is starting.", c.Make, c.Model)
}

// Implement the Stop method for Car
func (c Car) Stop() string {
    return fmt.Sprintf("%s %s is stopping.", c.Make, c.Model)
}

// Implement the Start method for Truck
func (t Truck) Start() string {
    return fmt.Sprintf("%s %s truck is starting with payload %d kg.", t.Make, t.Model,
t.Payload)
```

```go
}

// Implement the Stop method for Truck
func (t Truck) Stop() string {
    return fmt.Sprintf("%s %s truck is stopping.", t.Make, t.Model)
}

// Function to demonstrate polymorphism
func operateVehicle(v Vehicle) {
    fmt.Println(v.Start())
    fmt.Println(v.Stop())
}

func main() {
    car := Car{Make: "Toyota", Model: "Corolla"}
    truck := Truck{Make: "Ford", Model: "F-150", Payload: 1500}

    // Operate the vehicles
    operateVehicle(car)
    operateVehicle(truck)
}
```

Explanation:

- We define a Vehicle interface with two methods: Start() and Stop().
- The Car and Truck structs implement these methods.

- The operateVehicle() function demonstrates polymorphism by accepting any type that implements the Vehicle interface.
- The Car and Truck structs each have their own versions of the Start() and Stop() methods, but both conform to the same Vehicle interface.

Output:

csharp

Copy

```
Toyota Corolla is starting.
Toyota Corolla is stopping.
Ford F-150 truck is starting with payload 1500 kg.
Ford F-150 truck is stopping.
```

Summary of Practical Example:

- We modeled a **Vehicle** system using Go's OOP principles.
- We used **structs** to represent vehicles and **interfaces** to define common behavior.
- Each struct implemented its own version of methods like Start() and Stop, demonstrating **polymorphism**.

This simple application showcases how Go allows you to model real-world objects using **structs** and **interfaces** while adhering to object-oriented principles. The use of **composition**, **methods**, and **interfaces** helps keep the code modular, extensible, and easy to maintain.

In conclusion, Go provides the necessary tools to implement many key OOP principles, such as encapsulation, polymorphism, and abstraction, using structs and interfaces. Even though Go does not support traditional OOP features like inheritance, its simple and powerful model encourages a more compositional approach to building systems.

Chapter 11: Testing and Benchmarking Go Code

11.1 Why Testing Matters

Testing is an essential part of software development that helps ensure the correctness, reliability, and maintainability of your code. In Go, testing is highly encouraged, and the language's built-in testing tools make it easy to write tests and verify that your code behaves as expected.

Why Testing is Important:

1. **Early Bug Detection**: Writing tests helps you catch bugs early in the development process, ensuring that issues are identified before they become more difficult to fix.

2. **Improved Code Quality**: Writing tests forces you to write cleaner and more modular code. It encourages you to separate concerns and write functions that are easier to test.

3. **Regression Prevention**: As your application evolves, tests help ensure that new changes do not break existing functionality, preventing regressions in the codebase.

4. **Documentation**: Well-written tests serve as documentation for how the code is expected to behave. They help future developers (or yourself) understand the intended functionality of your code.

5. **Confidence in Refactoring**: When refactoring code, having a robust set of tests gives you confidence that your changes haven't inadvertently broken anything.

In Go, testing is integrated into the standard toolchain, making it simple and effective to add tests to your projects. Go's testing framework is built around the testing package, which provides functionality for writing unit tests, running them, and reporting the results.

11.2 Writing Unit Tests in Go

Unit testing in Go is straightforward and involves writing test functions that verify the behavior of your code. A **unit test** is designed to test a small, isolated part of your code, typically a single function or method. The goal is to ensure that the code behaves correctly for a variety of input values and edge cases.

Go's Testing Package

The core of Go's testing framework is the testing package. This package provides the necessary tools to write, run, and organize tests.

Basic Test Function

A test function in Go is simply a function that starts with the word Test followed by the name of the function being tested. It takes a single argument of type *testing.T, which is used to report failures.

Example: Basic Unit Test

go
Copy
```
package main

import "testing"
```

```go
// Function to be tested
func Add(a, b int) int {
    return a + b
}

// Unit test for Add function
func TestAdd(t *testing.T) {
    result := Add(2, 3)
    expected := 5
    if result != expected {
        t.Errorf("Add(2, 3) = %d; want %d", result, expected)
    }
}
```

Explanation:

- We define a simple function Add() that adds two integers.
- The test function TestAdd() checks whether Add(2, 3) returns 5 as expected. If the result doesn't match the expected value, we use t.Errorf() to report the failure.
- The *testing.T object provides methods like Errorf() and Fatalf() to log errors and failures during the test.

Running Tests

To run tests in Go, use the go test command in your terminal. This will search for files that end in _test.go and execute any functions that start with Test.

Command to run tests:

bash

Copy

go test

Example Output:

bash

Copy

$ go test

PASS

ok   example.com/project 0.002s

- If all tests pass, you will see PASS.
- If any test fails, you will see an error message detailing the failure.

You can also run tests for a specific file or function using:

bash

Copy

go test -run TestAdd

This will run only the TestAdd function.

Testing Multiple Cases with Table-Driven Tests

One of the best practices for writing unit tests in Go is using **table-driven tests**. This approach is useful for testing multiple input cases in a compact and readable manner. You define a table of test cases, each with input values and the expected result, and then loop through the cases to run the tests.

Example: Table-Driven Test

go
Copy

```go
package main

import "testing"

// Function to be tested
func Multiply(a, b int) int {
    return a * b
}

// Table-driven test for Multiply function
func TestMultiply(t *testing.T) {
    tests := []struct {
        a, b     int
        expected int
    }{
        {2, 3, 6},
```

```
        {4, 5, 20},
        {-1, -1, 1},
        {0, 10, 0},
    }

    for _, test := range tests {
        result := Multiply(test.a, test.b)
        if result != test.expected {
            t.Errorf("Multiply(%d, %d) = %d; want %d", test.a, test.b, result, test.expected)
        }
    }
}
```

Explanation:

- We define a table of test cases, where each test case contains two input values (a and b) and the expected result.
- The for loop iterates through each test case, calling the Multiply function and checking if the result matches the expected value.
- Table-driven tests are very common in Go because they make it easy to add new test cases and keep the test code organized.

Test Coverage

Go also provides a built-in way to measure test coverage. To see which parts of your code are being tested and which are not, you can use the -cover flag.

Command to run tests with coverage:

bash

Copy

go test -cover

This will show the percentage of your code that is covered by tests.

Example output with coverage:

bash

Copy

$ go test -cover

PASS

coverage: 100.0% of statements

ok   example.com/project 0.004s

If the coverage is less than 100%, you can use the -coverprofile flag to generate a more detailed report and analyze which parts of your code are not tested.

Command to generate a coverage profile:

bash

Copy

go test -coverprofile=coverage.out

You can then view the coverage report in your browser with the following command:

227

bash

Copy

```
go tool cover -html=coverage.out
```

This will open an HTML page with a detailed view of your code coverage.

Testing for Errors and Panics

You may also want to test that your functions handle errors or panic correctly.

Example: Testing for Errors

go

Copy

```go
package main

import (
    "errors"
    "testing"
)

func Divide(a, b int) (int, error) {
    if b == 0 {
        return 0, errors.New("cannot divide by zero")
    }
    return a / b, nil
}
```

228

```go
func TestDivide(t *testing.T) {
    _, err := Divide(4, 0)
    if err == nil {
        t.Error("Expected error, got nil")
    }
}
```

Explanation:

- The Divide() function returns an error if the divisor is zero.
- The test checks whether an error is returned when dividing by zero.

Example: Testing for Panic

go
Copy

```go
package main

import "testing"

func PanicFunction() {
    panic("something went wrong")
}

func TestPanicFunction(t *testing.T) {
    defer func() {
        if r := recover(); r == nil {
            t.Errorf("Expected panic, but got nil")
```

```
    }
}()
    PanicFunction()
}
```

Explanation:

- PanicFunction() intentionally causes a panic.
- The TestPanicFunction() test uses defer and recover() to catch the panic and verify that it occurs.

Summary of Writing Unit Tests:

- Go's testing package allows you to write unit tests to verify the correctness of your code.
- Tests are organized into functions that start with Test and accept a *testing.T argument.
- Table-driven tests are an effective way to test multiple cases in a clean and concise manner.
- You can run tests using go test and measure test coverage with the -cover flag.
- Go supports testing for errors, panics, and custom edge cases to ensure your functions handle unexpected situations properly.

By writing comprehensive unit tests, you ensure that your code is reliable, maintainable, and free from bugs. Go's simple testing framework makes it easy to get started and integrate tests into your workflow.

11.3 Benchmarking Go Code for Performance

Benchmarking is a key part of performance testing in Go. It allows you to measure how long a particular piece of code takes to execute, helping you identify bottlenecks and optimize performance. Go provides a built-in way to benchmark your code using the testing package, which enables you to write benchmarking functions alongside your unit tests.

Writing Benchmark Functions

Benchmark functions in Go are similar to test functions, but they measure the performance of code instead of checking correctness. A benchmark function has the following signature:

go
Copy
```go
func BenchmarkFunctionName(b *testing.B) { ... }
```

Where b is a pointer to testing.B, which provides methods for benchmarking, such as b.N, which indicates how many iterations the benchmark should run.

Example: Writing a Benchmark

Let's write a benchmark for a simple function that calculates the factorial of a number.

go
Copy
```go
package main
```

231

```go
import "testing"

// Factorial function to calculate the factorial of a number
func Factorial(n int) int {
    if n == 0 {
        return 1
    }
    return n * Factorial(n-1)
}

// Benchmark for the Factorial function
func BenchmarkFactorial(b *testing.B) {
    for i := 0; i < b.N; i++ {
        Factorial(10) // Benchmarking the factorial calculation for 10
    }
}
```

Explanation:

- We define a Factorial() function that calculates the factorial of a number recursively.
- The BenchmarkFactorial() function benchmarks Factorial(10) by running the function b.N times. The value of b.N is set by the testing framework to ensure a fair benchmark. The more iterations that are run, the more accurate the benchmark result will be.

Running Benchmarks

To run a benchmark, use the go test command with the -bench flag. The -bench flag allows you to specify a regular expression to run specific benchmarks or run all benchmarks in the package.

Command to run benchmarks:

bash
Copy
```
go test -bench .
```

Example Output:

bash
Copy
```
$ go test -bench .
BenchmarkFactorial-8    1000000    1053 ns/op
PASS
ok      example.com/project 0.002s
```

- The benchmark result shows that Factorial(10) takes **1053 nanoseconds** per operation (ns/op).
- The -8 after the benchmark name (BenchmarkFactorial-8) refers to the number of CPU cores used for the test (in this case, 8).
- The PASS message indicates that the benchmark completed successfully.

233

Benchmarking with Timer

You can also manually measure the time taken for specific operations using the testing.B object's StartTimer() and StopTimer() methods.

Example:

go
Copy

```go
package main

import (
    "testing"
    "time"
)

// Function to simulate a delay
func SimulateDelay() {
    time.Sleep(2 * time.Millisecond)
}

// Benchmark with manual timing
func BenchmarkSimulateDelay(b *testing.B) {
    b.ResetTimer() // Reset the timer to exclude setup time
    for i := 0; i < b.N; i++ {
        SimulateDelay() // Benchmark the SimulateDelay function
    }
}
```

234

Explanation:

- We use b.ResetTimer() to reset the benchmark timer, which ensures that only the code inside the loop is measured (excluding any setup time).
- The benchmark runs the SimulateDelay() function for b.N iterations, allowing us to measure its performance.

Profiling Benchmarks

Go also provides profiling capabilities through the pprof tool. This tool allows you to collect CPU and memory profiles while running your benchmarks, providing valuable insights into performance bottlenecks.

To profile your benchmark, use the -cpuprofile flag:

bash

Copy

```
go test -bench . -cpuprofile=cpu.prof
```

This will generate a CPU profile that you can analyze later. To visualize the profile, use the pprof tool:

bash

Copy

```
go tool pprof cpu.prof
```

This allows you to analyze how much CPU time was spent in each function and identify which parts of your code need optimization.

Summary of Benchmarking:

- Use testing.B to write benchmarking functions that measure the performance of your code.
- Run benchmarks with go test -bench to get execution time metrics like ns/op (nanoseconds per operation).
- Use b.ResetTimer() to measure only the operation being tested, excluding setup time.
- Profile benchmarks with pprof to gain insights into performance bottlenecks.

11.4 Practical Example: Writing Tests for Your Go Code

Let's now walk through a practical example of writing both unit tests and benchmarks for a simple Go application. We'll create a package that includes functions for adding, multiplying, and dividing numbers, and then we'll write tests to verify their behavior and benchmarks to measure performance.

Step 1: Creating the Functions

go
Copy
```
package mathops
```

```go
// Add function to add two integers
func Add(a, b int) int {
    return a + b
}

// Multiply function to multiply two integers
func Multiply(a, b int) int {
    return a * b
}

// Divide function to divide two integers and handle division by zero
func Divide(a, b int) (int, error) {
    if b == 0 {
        return 0, fmt.Errorf("cannot divide by zero")
    }
    return a / b, nil
}
```

Explanation:

- We define three functions: Add(), Multiply(), and Divide().
- Divide() handles division by zero by returning an error.

Step 2: Writing Unit Tests

Now, let's write unit tests for these functions using Go's testing framework.

go

237

Copy

```go
package mathops

import (
    "testing"
    "fmt"
)

func TestAdd(t *testing.T) {
    result := Add(2, 3)
    if result != 5 {
        t.Errorf("Add(2, 3) = %d; want 5", result)
    }
}

func TestMultiply(t *testing.T) {
    result := Multiply(3, 4)
    if result != 12 {
        t.Errorf("Multiply(3, 4) = %d; want 12", result)
    }
}

func TestDivide(t *testing.T) {
    result, err := Divide(10, 2)
    if err != nil {
        t.Errorf("Divide(10, 2) failed with error: %v", err)
    }
```

238

```go
    if result != 5 {
        t.Errorf("Divide(10, 2) = %d; want 5", result)
    }
}

func TestDivideByZero(t *testing.T) {
    _, err := Divide(10, 0)
    if err == nil {
        t.Errorf("Expected error, got nil")
    }
}
```

Explanation:

- We write tests for the Add(), Multiply(), and Divide() functions.
- The TestDivideByZero() function tests the error handling in the Divide() function when dividing by zero.
- We use t.Errorf() to report test failures if the result doesn't match the expected value.

Step 3: Writing Benchmarks

Now, let's write benchmarks for the Add(), Multiply(), and Divide() functions to measure their performance.

go

Copy

```go
package mathops
```

239

```go
import "testing"

func BenchmarkAdd(b *testing.B) {
    for i := 0; i < b.N; i++ {
        Add(2, 3)
    }
}

func BenchmarkMultiply(b *testing.B) {
    for i := 0; i < b.N; i++ {
        Multiply(3, 4)
    }
}

func BenchmarkDivide(b *testing.B) {
    for i := 0; i < b.N; i++ {
        Divide(10, 2)
    }
}
```

Explanation:

- Each benchmark function runs the respective function (Add(), Multiply(), Divide()) b.N times.
- The Go testing framework will automatically adjust b.N to get statistically significant results.

240

Step 4: Running Tests and Benchmarks

To run the tests and benchmarks, you can use the following commands:

Run Unit Tests:

bash

Copy

```
go test
```

1. **Run Benchmarks**:

   bash

   Copy

   ```
   go test -bench .
   ```

2. **Example Output for Tests:**

bash

Copy

```
$ go test
PASS
ok      example.com/project 0.002s
```

Example Output for Benchmarks:

bash

Copy

```
$ go test -bench .
BenchmarkAdd-8          10000000    100 ns/op
BenchmarkMultiply-8     10000000    50 ns/op
```

```
BenchmarkDivide-8    5000000    150 ns/op
PASS
ok    example.com/project 1.000s
```

Explanation:

- The benchmarks show how long each function took to execute, measured in **nanoseconds per operation** (ns/op).
- The higher the number of iterations, the more reliable the benchmark result will be.

Summary of Writing Tests and Benchmarks:

- Unit tests help you verify the correctness of your functions and ensure they behave as expected under different conditions.
- Benchmarks allow you to measure the performance of your functions, helping you identify areas for optimization.
- Go's testing framework makes it easy to write and run both tests and benchmarks, giving you confidence in both the correctness and performance of your code.

By incorporating both tests and benchmarks into your development process, you ensure that your code is not only correct but also efficient, leading to higher-quality, maintainable applications.

242

Chapter 12: Advanced Topics

12.1 Go and Databases: Connecting to SQL and NoSQL Databases

Databases are essential components of modern applications, whether you're storing user data, application configurations, or complex relational data. In Go, you can interact with both SQL and NoSQL databases through libraries and drivers that provide a seamless connection to these database systems. This section will focus on how to connect to both SQL (such as MySQL, PostgreSQL) and NoSQL (such as MongoDB) databases in Go.

SQL Databases in Go

Go supports working with SQL databases via the database/sql package. This package provides a generic interface for interacting with different relational databases.

Steps to Connect to a SQL Database in Go:

1. **Install the appropriate driver**: Go does not include a built-in driver for any specific database, so you need to install a third-party package to interact with your chosen SQL database.
   - For PostgreSQL: github.com/lib/pq
   - For MySQL: github.com/go-sql-driver/mysql
2. **Establish a connection**: Use the sql.Open() function to establish a connection to the database.
3. **Querying the database**: You can use functions like Query(), QueryRow(), and Exec() to interact with the database.
4. **Closing the connection**: Always close your database connection to free up resources.

Example: Connecting to a MySQL Database

go

Copy

```go
package main

import (
    "database/sql"
    "fmt"
    "log"

    _ "github.com/go-sql-driver/mysql"
)

func main() {
    // Establishing a connection to the MySQL database
    db, err := sql.Open("mysql", "user:password@tcp(localhost:3306)/dbname")
    if err != nil {
        log.Fatal(err)
    }
    defer db.Close()

    // Test the database connection
    err = db.Ping()
    if err != nil {
        log.Fatal(err)
```

244

```go
    }
    fmt.Println("Successfully connected to the database!")

    // Perform a query
    rows, err := db.Query("SELECT name, age FROM users")
    if err != nil {
        log.Fatal(err)
    }
    defer rows.Close()

    for rows.Next() {
        var name string
        var age int
        err := rows.Scan(&name, &age)
        if err != nil {
            log.Fatal(err)
        }
        fmt.Printf("%s is %d years old\n", name, age)
    }

    // Check for errors from iterating over rows
    err = rows.Err()
    if err != nil {
        log.Fatal(err)
    }
}
```

Explanation:

- sql.Open() opens a new connection to the database. It's essential to use a driver such as github.com/go-sql-driver/mysql to connect to MySQL.
- db.Ping() verifies that the connection to the database is established.
- db.Query() is used to run a SQL query, and rows.Scan() reads the result into variables.

NoSQL Databases in Go

Go also supports working with NoSQL databases like MongoDB and Redis, offering flexibility in handling unstructured or semi-structured data.

Example: Connecting to MongoDB in Go

To interact with MongoDB, you need the go.mongodb.org/mongo-driver/mongo package.

Install MongoDB driver:

bash

Copy

go get go.mongodb.org/mongo-driver/mongo

1. **Example of Connecting to MongoDB:**

go

Copy

```
package main

import (
    "context"
```

```go
	"fmt"
	"log"
	"time"

	"go.mongodb.org/mongo-driver/bson"
	"go.mongodb.org/mongo-driver/mongo"
	"go.mongodb.org/mongo-driver/mongo/options"
)

func main() {
	// Create a new MongoDB client
	clientOptions := options.Client().ApplyURI("mongodb://localhost:27017")
	client, err := mongo.Connect(context.TODO(), clientOptions)
	if err != nil {
		log.Fatal(err)
	}
	defer client.Disconnect(context.TODO())

	// Verify the connection
	err = client.Ping(context.TODO(), nil)
	if err != nil {
		log.Fatal(err)
	}
	fmt.Println("Successfully connected to MongoDB!")

	// Access a collection
	collection := client.Database("testdb").Collection("users")
```

```go
// Insert a document
user := bson.D{{"name", "Alice"}, {"age", 30}}
_, err = collection.InsertOne(context.TODO(), user)
if err != nil {
    log.Fatal(err)
}
fmt.Println("Inserted a document")

// Find a document
var result bson.D
err = collection.FindOne(context.TODO(), bson.D{{"name",
"Alice"}}).Decode(&result)
if err != nil {
    log.Fatal(err)
}
fmt.Printf("Found document: %v\n", result)
}
```

Explanation:

- We connect to MongoDB using the MongoDB Go driver.
- We insert a document into the users collection in the testdb database.
- We use FindOne() to retrieve a document from the collection.

Summary of Database Interaction in Go:

- Go supports both **SQL** and **NoSQL** databases with simple, efficient packages.
- The database/sql package is used for SQL databases, and you need to install specific drivers for each database (e.g., MySQL, PostgreSQL).
- NoSQL databases like MongoDB can be accessed through their respective Go drivers.
- Always close database connections after use to free resources.

12.2 Go Routines for Parallel Processing

Go's concurrency model, based on **goroutines**, is one of the language's most powerful features. Goroutines allow you to run functions concurrently, making Go an excellent choice for parallel processing tasks, such as handling multiple HTTP requests, performing calculations, or processing data in parallel.

A **goroutine** is a lightweight thread of execution. They are managed by the Go runtime, and you can start a new goroutine using the go keyword.

Starting a Goroutine

To start a goroutine, simply prepend a function call with the go keyword. This causes the function to run concurrently with the rest of your program.

Example: Basic Goroutine

go
Copy
package main

```go
import (
    "fmt"
    "time"
)

func printMessage(message string) {
    time.Sleep(2 * time.Second)
    fmt.Println(message)
}

func main() {
    // Start a goroutine
    go printMessage("Hello from Goroutine!")

    // The main function continues running concurrently
    fmt.Println("Main function running")

    // Give the goroutine time to finish before the main function exits
    time.Sleep(3 * time.Second)
}
```

Explanation:

- The go printMessage("Hello from Goroutine!") starts a goroutine that prints the message after a 2-second delay.
- The main function continues running concurrently, printing "Main function running".

- time.Sleep(3 * time.Second) is used to give the goroutine enough time to complete before the main function exits.

Goroutines and Synchronization

While goroutines are powerful, they often require **synchronization** when accessing shared resources or when waiting for multiple goroutines to finish executing. Go provides several synchronization mechanisms, such as **channels** and the **sync package**, to handle this.

Example: Synchronizing Goroutines with WaitGroup

A sync.WaitGroup allows you to wait for a collection of goroutines to finish executing. You use Add() to specify how many goroutines to wait for, Done() when each goroutine finishes, and Wait() to block until all goroutines are done.

go
Copy

```
package main

import (
    "fmt"
    "sync"
    "time"
)

func printMessage(message string, wg *sync.WaitGroup) {
    defer wg.Done() // Notify that this goroutine is done
    time.Sleep(2 * time.Second)
```

```
    fmt.Println(message)
}

func main() {
    var wg sync.WaitGroup

    // Start multiple goroutines
    wg.Add(2) // We have two goroutines to wait for
    go printMessage("Hello from Goroutine 1!", &wg)
    go printMessage("Hello from Goroutine 2!", &wg)

    // Wait for all goroutines to finish
    wg.Wait()
    fmt.Println("All goroutines finished")
}
```

Explanation:

- wg.Add(2) tells the WaitGroup that we have two goroutines to wait for.
- defer wg.Done() in the printMessage function ensures that once the function finishes, it notifies the WaitGroup.
- wg.Wait() blocks until both goroutines are finished.

Channels: Communication Between Goroutines

252

In Go, **channels** provide a way for goroutines to communicate with each other. You can send and receive values through channels, making it easier to share data between goroutines.

Example: Using Channels to Communicate Between Goroutines

go
Copy

```
package main

import (
    "fmt"
)

func calculateSquare(n int, ch chan int) {
    result := n * n
    ch <- result // Send result to the channel
}

func main() {
    ch := make(chan int)

    // Start a goroutine to calculate the square of 5
    go calculateSquare(5, ch)

    // Receive the result from the channel
    result := <-ch
    fmt.Println("The square is:", result)
```

253

```
}
```

Explanation:

- We create a channel `ch` to send data between the `main` function and the goroutine.
- The `calculateSquare` function calculates the square of a number and sends the result back to the channel.
- The `main` function receives the result from the channel and prints it.

Summary of Goroutines:

- **Goroutines** allow you to run functions concurrently, enabling parallel processing in Go.
- **WaitGroups** can be used to wait for multiple goroutines to finish.
- **Channels** provide a way for goroutines to communicate and share data safely.
- Go's concurrency model, based on goroutines and channels, allows you to write highly efficient and concurrent applications with minimal complexity.

Go's built-in support for database interaction and parallel processing with goroutines makes it an excellent choice for building high-performance, concurrent applications. Whether you are connecting to SQL and NoSQL databases or managing concurrent tasks with goroutines, Go's simplicity and efficiency shine through. By leveraging these advanced topics, you can build scalable, robust applications that meet the demands of modern systems.

12.3 Advanced Error Handling Strategies

Error handling is a crucial aspect of writing reliable and maintainable Go code. While Go's approach to error handling, which relies on explicitly checking error values, is simple and straightforward, there are advanced techniques you can use to handle errors more effectively in complex applications. This section explores some advanced strategies for error handling in Go that can help improve the readability, efficiency, and maintainability of your code.

1. Wrapping Errors for Context

In Go, errors are typically returned as values that provide a message about what went wrong. However, as your application grows, it might be necessary to provide more context about an error. The fmt.Errorf() function, introduced in Go 1.13, allows you to wrap errors with additional context.

Example: Wrapping an Error

go

Copy

```
package main

import (

    "fmt"

    "errors"
```

```go
)

func processFile(fileName string) error {
    if fileName == "" {
        return fmt.Errorf("processFile failed: %w", errors.New("file name cannot be empty"))
    }
    // Process the file...
    return nil
}

func main() {
    err := processFile("")
    if err != nil {
        fmt.Println("Error:", err) // Error: processFile failed: file name cannot be empty
    }
}
```

Explanation:

- The fmt.Errorf() function allows you to add context to an error by wrapping it with the %w verb. This makes it easier to understand where and why the error occurred.

2. Error Unwrapping

When you wrap errors, you can also "unwrap" them to access the original error, which can be useful if you need to check for specific errors. The errors.Is() and errors.As() functions, introduced in Go 1.13, provide ways to inspect and match specific errors.

Example: Unwrapping an Error

go

Copy

```go
package main

import (

    "fmt"

    "errors"

)


var ErrFileNotFound = errors.New("file not found")
```

```go
func readFile(fileName string) error {

    if fileName == "" {

        return fmt.Errorf("readFile failed: %w", ErrFileNotFound)

    }

    // Read the file...

    return nil

}


func main() {

    err := readFile("")

    if err != nil {

        if errors.Is(err, ErrFileNotFound) {

            fmt.Println("Custom Error: File not found")

        } else {

            fmt.Println("Error:", err)

        }
```

```
        }

    }
```

Explanation:

- errors.Is() checks whether the error matches a specific error (ErrFileNotFound) that was wrapped inside another error.
- This allows for more fine-grained error handling, where you can decide what action to take depending on the type or context of the error.

3. Using Sentinel Errors

A **sentinel error** is a predefined error value that you can compare against to indicate specific conditions in your code. These errors are often used in Go to signal well-known error conditions, such as file not found or invalid input.

Example: Sentinel Error

go

Copy

```
package main

import (

    "fmt"
```

```go
	"errors"

)


var ErrInvalidInput = errors.New("invalid input")


func processInput(input string) error {

	if input == "" {

		return ErrInvalidInput

	}

	// Process input...

	return nil

}


func main() {

	err := processInput("")

	if err != nil {

		if errors.Is(err, ErrInvalidInput) {
```

```go
        fmt.Println("Sentinel Error: Invalid input provided")

    } else {

        fmt.Println("Error:", err)

    }

}

}
```

Explanation:

- ErrInvalidInput is a sentinel error. In this case, we compare the returned error against the predefined error value to handle a specific case of invalid input.

4. Custom Error Types

While Go's default error handling works for many use cases, sometimes you may need more flexibility. In such cases, creating **custom error types** can help. A custom error type can include additional fields and methods that provide more context about the error.

Example: Custom Error Type

go

Copy

```go
package main
```

261

```go
import "fmt"


// Custom error type with additional context

type FileError struct {

    Op  string // Operation that failed (e.g., "open", "read")

    File string // File that caused the error

    Err  error  // Underlying error

}


// Implement the error interface for FileError

func (e *FileError) Error() string {

    return fmt.Sprintf("FileError: %s %s: %v", e.Op, e.File, e.Err)

}


func readFile(fileName string) error {

    if fileName == "" {
```

```go
    return &FileError{

        Op:   "read",

        File: fileName,

        Err:  fmt.Errorf("file name cannot be empty"),

    }

}

// Read the file...

    return nil

}


func main() {

    err := readFile("")

    if err != nil {

        fmt.Println("Error:", err)  // Output: FileError: read : file name cannot be empty

    }

}
```

Explanation:

263

- FileError is a custom error type that includes additional fields (Op, File, and Err).
- By implementing the Error() method, the FileError type satisfies the error interface.
- This custom error type provides more detailed information, which is useful for debugging.

Summary of Advanced Error Handling:

- Use **error wrapping** with fmt.Errorf() to add context to errors.
- **Unwrap errors** with errors.Is() and errors.As() to examine the underlying error.
- **Sentinel errors** provide predefined error values to signal specific conditions.
- **Custom error types** allow you to add more context to errors by attaching additional fields and methods.

By applying these advanced error handling strategies, you can make your Go code more robust, readable, and easier to debug.

12.4 Performance Optimization Tips and Techniques

Optimizing the performance of Go applications is important for ensuring that they run efficiently, especially in large-scale systems. Go provides a number of built-in tools and techniques for identifying performance bottlenecks and optimizing code. In this section, we'll explore some essential tips and techniques to help you optimize your Go code.

1. Use the pprof Package for Profiling

Go has a built-in package called pprof for profiling your application. It allows you to collect and analyze CPU, memory, and block profiles, providing insights into which parts of your code are taking the most time or consuming the most memory.

Example: Enabling CPU Profiling

go

Copy

```
package main

import (
    "fmt"

    "log"

    "net/http"

    "net/http/pprof"

    "os"

    "runtime/pprof"
)


func main() {
```

265

```go
// Create a CPU profile file

f, err := os.Create("cpu_profile.prof")

if err != nil {

    log.Fatal(err)

}

defer f.Close()


// Start CPU profiling

if err := pprof.StartCPUProfile(f); err != nil {

    log.Fatal(err)

}

defer pprof.StopCPUProfile()


// Simulate some work

fmt.Println("Starting work...")

for i := 0; i < 10000000; i++ {

    _ = i * i // Simulated work
```

```
    }

    // Register pprof handlers

    http.HandleFunc("/debug/pprof/", pprof.Index)

    log.Fatal(http.ListenAndServe(":8080", nil))

}
```

Explanation:

- pprof.StartCPUProfile(f) starts profiling and saves the CPU profile to a file.
- pprof.StopCPUProfile() stops profiling when the program finishes.
- This can help you identify which parts of your program are consuming the most CPU time.

To view the profile data, use the go tool pprof command:

bash

Copy

```
go tool pprof cpu_profile.prof
```

This will open an interactive interface where you can analyze the CPU profile.

267

2. Avoid Unnecessary Memory Allocations

In Go, memory allocations can be expensive in terms of both time and space. Optimizing memory allocation is essential for performance, particularly when handling large datasets or high-throughput applications.

Techniques for Avoiding Unnecessary Allocations:

- **Reuse buffers**: Use sync.Pool to reuse memory buffers instead of allocating new ones repeatedly.
- **Preallocate slices**: When working with slices, preallocate their capacity to avoid resizing during runtime.

Example: Preallocating a Slice

go

Copy

```
package main

import "fmt"

func main() {
    // Preallocate a slice with sufficient capacity
    nums := make([]int, 0, 100) // Capacity of 100
```

268

```
for i := 0; i < 100; i++ {

    nums = append(nums, i)

}

fmt.Println(nums)

}
```

Explanation:

- By preallocating the slice with a capacity of 100, we avoid reallocations as the slice grows.

3. Optimize Garbage Collection (GC)

Go's garbage collector (GC) automatically reclaims memory, but it can introduce pauses during execution. You can optimize garbage collection by reducing the number of allocations and deallocations in your code.

Tips for Reducing GC Impact:

- **Minimize allocations**: Use stack-allocated variables whenever possible and avoid unnecessary object creation.
- **Control GC behavior**: Use environment variables like GOGC to control the frequency of garbage collection cycles.

Example: Setting GOGC

bash

Copy

```
GOGC=100 go run your_program.go
```

The GOGC environment variable controls the garbage collection trigger threshold. A lower value causes more frequent GC cycles, while a higher value reduces the frequency.

4. Use Efficient Data Structures

The choice of data structures can significantly affect the performance of your application. Go offers several built-in data structures, but in some cases, custom data structures might be more efficient.

- **Slices** are efficient for sequential data but might not be suitable for certain operations like inserting in the middle of a collection.
- **Maps** are great for fast lookups but may have overhead when managing large amounts of data.
- Consider using **binary search trees** or **hash tables** for complex data storage and retrieval operations.

5. Concurrency for Performance

270

Go's concurrency model, based on goroutines and channels, allows you to efficiently utilize multiple CPU cores. By dividing a task into smaller parts and processing them concurrently, you can significantly improve performance.

Example: Using Goroutines for Concurrent Processing

go

Copy

```go
package main

import (

    "fmt"

    "sync"

)

func processData(data int, wg *sync.WaitGroup) {

    defer wg.Done()

    fmt.Printf("Processing data: %d\n", data)

}


func main() {

    var wg sync.WaitGroup
```

```
data := []int{1, 2, 3, 4, 5}

for _, d := range data {

    wg.Add(1)

    go processData(d, &wg)

}


wg.Wait()

}
```

Explanation:

- We use goroutines to process each piece of data concurrently, and the
  sync.WaitGroup ensures that the program waits for all goroutines to finish before
  exiting.

6. Use Efficient Libraries and Packages

Make sure to leverage well-optimized third-party libraries when possible. Libraries like
gorilla/mux for routing or go-redis/redis for Redis clients are designed to be efficient
and easy to use.

Summary of Performance Optimization:

272

- Use **profiling** tools like pprof to identify bottlenecks.
- **Avoid unnecessary memory allocations** by reusing objects and preallocating memory where possible.
- **Optimize garbage collection** by minimizing allocations and adjusting the GC behavior using GOGC.
- Choose the right **data structures** for your application's needs.
- Use **concurrency** with goroutines and channels to parallelize tasks and improve performance.
- Utilize **efficient libraries** to avoid reinventing the wheel.

By applying these techniques, you can significantly improve the performance of your Go applications and ensure they can handle high throughput and large datasets effectively.

Chapter 13: Building Projects in Go

13.1 Creating Your First Project: A To-Do List Application

One of the best ways to learn a new programming language is by building something useful. In this section, we'll create a simple **To-Do List Application** using Go. This application will allow the user to add, list, and delete tasks. We'll also use a text file for persistent storage so that tasks can be saved even after the application is closed.

Step 1: Define the Project Structure

First, let's define the structure of our project. Our To-Do list app will consist of the following files:

go
Copy

```
todo-app/
    |- main.go        // The main Go file for running the app
    |- tasks.txt      // A text file for storing tasks
```

Step 2: Writing the Go Code

Let's start by writing the main logic of the To-Do application. We will provide the ability to:

- Add tasks
- List all tasks
- Delete tasks

main.go

go
Copy
```go
package main

import (
    "fmt"
    "io/ioutil"
    "os"
    "strings"
)

func readTasks() ([]string, error) {
    data, err := ioutil.ReadFile("tasks.txt")
    if err != nil {
        if os.IsNotExist(err) {
            return []string{}, nil // No tasks file exists, return empty slice
        }
        return nil, err
    }
    tasks := strings.Split(string(data), "\n")
    return tasks, nil
}

func saveTasks(tasks []string) error {
    data := strings.Join(tasks, "\n")
```

```go
    return ioutil.WriteFile("tasks.txt", []byte(data), 0644)
}

func addTask(task string) error {
    tasks, err := readTasks()
    if err != nil {
        return err
    }
    tasks = append(tasks, task)
    return saveTasks(tasks)
}

func deleteTask(index int) error {
    tasks, err := readTasks()
    if err != nil {
        return err
    }
    if index < 0 || index >= len(tasks) {
        return fmt.Errorf("task index out of range")
    }
    tasks = append(tasks[:index], tasks[index+1:]...)
    return saveTasks(tasks)
}

func listTasks() error {
    tasks, err := readTasks()
    if err != nil {
```

```go
        return err
    }
    if len(tasks) == 0 {
        fmt.Println("No tasks to display.")
        return nil
    }
    fmt.Println("To-Do List:")
    for i, task := range tasks {
        fmt.Printf("%d: %s\n", i+1, task)
    }
    return nil
}

func main() {
    fmt.Println("Welcome to the To-Do List App")
    for {
        fmt.Println("\n1. Add Task")
        fmt.Println("2. List Tasks")
        fmt.Println("3. Delete Task")
        fmt.Println("4. Exit")
        fmt.Print("Choose an option: ")

        var option int
        _, err := fmt.Scan(&option)
        if err != nil {
            fmt.Println("Invalid input. Please choose a valid option.")
            continue
```

```go
    }

    switch option {
    case 1:
        fmt.Print("Enter the task description: ")
        var task string
        fmt.Scan(&task)
        if err := addTask(task); err != nil {
            fmt.Println("Error adding task:", err)
        } else {
            fmt.Println("Task added!")
        }
    case 2:
        if err := listTasks(); err != nil {
            fmt.Println("Error listing tasks:", err)
        }
    case 3:
        fmt.Print("Enter task number to delete: ")
        var taskNum int
        fmt.Scan(&taskNum)
        if err := deleteTask(taskNum - 1); err != nil {
            fmt.Println("Error deleting task:", err)
        } else {
            fmt.Println("Task deleted!")
        }
    case 4:
        fmt.Println("Exiting...")
```

```
        return
    default:
        fmt.Println("Invalid option, please choose a valid option.")
    }
  }
}
```

Explanation of the Code:

1. **readTasks()**: Reads the list of tasks from the tasks.txt file and returns it as a slice of strings.
2. **saveTasks()**: Writes the list of tasks to the tasks.txt file.
3. **addTask()**: Appends a new task to the task list and saves it.
4. **deleteTask()**: Deletes a task by its index from the task list and saves the updated list.
5. **listTasks()**: Displays all the tasks in the terminal.
6. **main()**: Provides a simple menu interface for interacting with the To-Do List application. The user can add tasks, list tasks, or delete tasks.

Step 3: Running the Application

1. Create a new directory for your project and save the main.go file in it.
2. Open a terminal and navigate to your project directory.

Run the Go application with the following command:

bash

Copy

go run main.go

279

3. The application will prompt you with a simple text-based interface where you can add tasks, list tasks, or delete tasks.

Example Interaction:

mathematica

Copy

Welcome to the To-Do List App

1. Add Task
2. List Tasks
3. Delete Task
4. Exit
Choose an option: 1
Enter the task description: Buy groceries
Task added!

Welcome to the To-Do List App

1. Add Task
2. List Tasks
3. Delete Task
4. Exit
Choose an option: 2
To-Do List:
1: Buy groceries

This is a simple but effective To-Do list application in Go. You can extend this application by adding features like task deadlines, priorities, or different task statuses (e.g., "Completed", "Pending").

13.2 Building a Command-Line Tool

Command-line tools are incredibly useful for automating tasks, interacting with servers, or managing files. Go makes it easy to build command-line tools thanks to its powerful standard library and simple syntax. In this section, we will build a simple **command-line tool** that allows users to interact with files in a directory.

Step 1: Define the Project Structure

Let's define a basic project structure for our command-line tool:

```
go
Copy
file-cli/
   |- main.go      // The main Go file for the tool
```

Step 2: Writing the Go Code

In this example, our command-line tool will:

- List the contents of a directory.
- Create a new file.
- Delete a file.

281

main.go

go
Copy
```go
package main

import (
    "fmt"
    "os"
    "path/filepath"
    "log"
)

func listFiles(path string) error {
    files, err := os.ReadDir(path)
    if err != nil {
        return err
    }
    for _, file := range files {
        fmt.Println(file.Name())
    }
    return nil
}

func createFile(filePath string) error {
    file, err := os.Create(filePath)
    if err != nil {
```

```go
        return err
    }
    defer file.Close()
    fmt.Println("File created:", filePath)
    return nil
}

func deleteFile(filePath string) error {
    err := os.Remove(filePath)
    if err != nil {
        return err
    }
    fmt.Println("File deleted:", filePath)
    return nil
}

func main() {
    fmt.Println("Welcome to the File CLI Tool")
    for {
        fmt.Println("\n1. List Files in Directory")
        fmt.Println("2. Create a New File")
        fmt.Println("3. Delete a File")
        fmt.Println("4. Exit")
        fmt.Print("Choose an option: ")

        var option int
        _, err := fmt.Scan(&option)
```

```go
if err != nil {
    fmt.Println("Invalid input. Please choose a valid option.")
    continue
}

switch option {
case 1:
    fmt.Print("Enter the directory path: ")
    var path string
    fmt.Scan(&path)
    if err := listFiles(path); err != nil {
        fmt.Println("Error:", err)
    }
case 2:
    fmt.Print("Enter the file path to create: ")
    var path string
    fmt.Scan(&path)
    if err := createFile(path); err != nil {
        fmt.Println("Error:", err)
    }
case 3:
    fmt.Print("Enter the file path to delete: ")
    var path string
    fmt.Scan(&path)
    if err := deleteFile(path); err != nil {
        fmt.Println("Error:", err)
    }
```

```
case 4:
    fmt.Println("Exiting...")
    return
default:
    fmt.Println("Invalid option, please choose a valid option.")
    }
  }
}
```

Explanation of the Code:

1. **listFiles()**: Lists all the files in the provided directory.
2. **createFile()**: Creates a new file at the provided path.
3. **deleteFile()**: Deletes the specified file.
4. **main()**: Provides a simple menu for interacting with the command-line tool. The user can list files, create new files, or delete files.

Step 3: Running the Command-Line Tool

1. Create a new directory for your project and save the main.go file in it.
2. Open a terminal and navigate to your project directory.

Run the Go application with the following command:

bash

Copy

go run main.go

3. You will see a menu where you can choose to list files in a directory, create a new file, or delete a file.

Example Interaction:

mathematica

Copy

Welcome to the File CLI Tool

1. List Files in Directory
2. Create a New File
3. Delete a File
4. Exit
Choose an option: 1
Enter the directory path: .
file1.txt
file2.txt
file3.txt

This is a simple command-line tool that interacts with the filesystem. You can extend it by adding features like renaming files, moving files, or searching for files.

---

we created two different types of Go applications:

1. A **To-Do List Application**: A basic project where we built a to-do list with functionality to add, list, and delete tasks, along with file persistence.

2. **A Command-Line Tool**: A CLI tool for interacting with files in a directory, allowing the user to list, create, and delete files.

By building projects like these, you can familiarize yourself with Go's syntax, libraries, and file handling, as well as learn how to build useful tools and applications efficiently.

13.3 Building a Web Scraper with Go

Web scraping is the process of extracting data from websites. It is widely used for tasks such as collecting information from e-commerce websites, news sites, or blogs. In Go, web scraping can be accomplished using libraries like net/http for making HTTP requests, goquery for parsing HTML, and strings for working with text. In this section, we'll create a simple **web scraper** that collects headlines from a news website.

Step 1: Define the Project Structure

Our web scraper project will look like this:

go

Copy

```
web-scraper/

    |- main.go        // The Go file for the scraper
```

Step 2: Installing Dependencies

To scrape websites, we need the goquery package, which is a popular Go library that makes it easy to parse HTML documents and extract data. You can install goquery using go get.

bash

Copy

```
go get github.com/PuerkitoBio/goquery
```

Step 3: Writing the Go Code for Scraping

In this example, we'll scrape the headlines from a news website like BBC or CNN.

main.go

go

Copy

```
package main

import (
    "fmt"
    "log"
    "net/http"
```

288

```go
    "github.com/PuerkitoBio/goquery"
)


func scrapeHeadlines(url string) ([]string, error) {
    // Make an HTTP request to get the webpage
    res, err := http.Get(url)
    if err != nil {
        return nil, fmt.Errorf("failed to fetch the page: %w", err)
    }
    defer res.Body.Close()


    // Parse the HTML response
    doc, err := goquery.NewDocumentFromReader(res.Body)
    if err != nil {
        return nil, fmt.Errorf("failed to parse the HTML: %w", err)
    }
```

289

```go
	// Find the headlines using CSS selectors
	var headlines []string
	doc.Find(".gs-c-promo-heading__title").Each(func(i int, s *goquery.Selection) {
		headline := s.Text()
		headlines = append(headlines, headline)
	})

	return headlines, nil
}


func main() {
	url := "https://www.bbc.com/news" // Example website to scrape

	headlines, err := scrapeHeadlines(url)
	if err != nil {
		log.Fatal(err)
	}
```

```go
fmt.Println("Headlines from BBC News:")

for _, headline := range headlines {

    fmt.Println(headline)

}

}
```

Explanation of the Code:

1. **scrapeHeadlines()**: This function takes a URL as input, makes an HTTP request to fetch the page, and then uses the goquery library to parse the HTML. It looks for the HTML elements that contain the headlines using CSS selectors (.gs-c-promo-heading__title in this case for BBC) and appends each headline to the headlines slice.

2. **main()**: The main() function sets the target URL (BBC News in this case), calls the scrapeHeadlines() function, and prints each headline found on the page.

Step 4: Running the Web Scraper

1. Create a new directory for your project and save the main.go file in it.

2. Open a terminal and navigate to your project directory.

Run the scraper with the following command:

bash

Copy

```
go run main.go
```

3. You should see a list of headlines from the BBC News website printed in your terminal.

Example Output:

python

Copy

```
Headlines from BBC News:

Scotland voters divided over independence, poll finds

US Capitol riot: Donald Trump incited violence, House says

US stocks rise after turbulent week

...
```

Tips for Scraping:

- **Respect robots.txt**: Always check a website's robots.txt file to ensure scraping is allowed.
- **Be careful with the frequency**: Don't overwhelm websites with frequent requests, as it may lead to being blocked or throttled.

13.4 A Final Project: A Simple Web Server with CRUD Functionality

In this section, we will build a simple **web server** with **CRUD** (Create, Read, Update, Delete) functionality. This web server will manage a list of tasks, similar to a To-Do list application, but using a more structured approach with HTTP endpoints.

Step 1: Define the Project Structure

Our project structure will look like this:

less

Copy

```
todo-web/
    |- main.go      // Go file for the web server
    |- tasks.json   // File to store the tasks in JSON format
```

Step 2: Writing the Go Code for the Web Server

In this example, we will use the net/http package to create a simple web server and the encoding/json package to handle JSON data for storing tasks.

main.go

go

Copy

```go
package main

import (
    "encoding/json"

    "fmt"

    "log"

    "net/http"

    "os"

    "sync"
)


var tasks []string
var mu sync.Mutex


func loadTasks() error {
    file, err := os.Open("tasks.json")
```

```go
    if err != nil {

        return err

    }

    defer file.Close()


    decoder := json.NewDecoder(file)

    err = decoder.Decode(&tasks)

    return err

}


func saveTasks() error {

    file, err := os.Create("tasks.json")

    if err != nil {

        return err

    }

    defer file.Close()
```

```go
    encoder := json.NewEncoder(file)

    err = encoder.Encode(tasks)

    return err

}


func getTasks(w http.ResponseWriter, r *http.Request) {

    mu.Lock()

    defer mu.Unlock()

    w.Header().Set("Content-Type", "application/json")

    json.NewEncoder(w).Encode(tasks)

}


func addTask(w http.ResponseWriter, r *http.Request) {

    mu.Lock()

    defer mu.Unlock()


    var task string
```

```go
    if err := json.NewDecoder(r.Body).Decode(&task); err != nil {

        http.Error(w, "Invalid task", http.StatusBadRequest)

        return

    }

    tasks = append(tasks, task)

    saveTasks()


    w.WriteHeader(http.StatusCreated)

    fmt.Fprintf(w, "Task added")

}


func deleteTask(w http.ResponseWriter, r *http.Request) {

    mu.Lock()

    defer mu.Unlock()


    var taskIndex int

    if err := json.NewDecoder(r.Body).Decode(&taskIndex); err != nil {
```

```go
        http.Error(w, "Invalid index", http.StatusBadRequest)

        return

    }


    if taskIndex < 0 || taskIndex >= len(tasks) {

        http.Error(w, "Task not found", http.StatusNotFound)

        return

    }


    tasks = append(tasks[:taskIndex], tasks[taskIndex+1:]...)

    saveTasks()


    fmt.Fprintf(w, "Task deleted")

}


func main() {

    if err := loadTasks(); err != nil {
```

```
        log.Fatal("Error loading tasks:", err)

    }


    http.HandleFunc("/tasks", getTasks)

    http.HandleFunc("/tasks/add", addTask)

    http.HandleFunc("/tasks/delete", deleteTask)


    fmt.Println("Starting web server on :8080...")

    log.Fatal(http.ListenAndServe(":8080", nil))

}
```

Explanation of the Code:

1. **loadTasks() and saveTasks()**: These functions read from and write to a file (tasks.json) to persist the tasks between server restarts. JSON is used to store and retrieve tasks.
2. **getTasks()**: This function handles GET requests to fetch the list of tasks. It returns the tasks in JSON format.
3. **addTask()**: This function handles POST requests to add a new task to the list. It reads the task from the request body and appends it to the task list.

4. **deleteTask()**: This function handles DELETE requests to remove a task by its index. The index is provided in the request body.
5. **main()**: The main() function starts an HTTP server that listens on port 8080. It registers routes for adding, listing, and deleting tasks.

Step 3: Running the Web Server

1. Create a new directory for your project and save the main.go file in it.
2. Create an empty tasks.json file to store the tasks.
3. Open a terminal and navigate to your project directory.

Run the web server:
bash
Copy

```
go run main.go
```

4.

The server will start and listen for requests at http://localhost:8080.

Step 4: Testing the Web Server

You can interact with the web server using tools like curl or Postman.

List all tasks:
bash
Copy

```
curl http://localhost:8080/tasks
```

1. **Add a new task**:
   bash

300

Copy

```
curl -X POST -d '"Learn Go"' http://localhost:8080/tasks/add
```

2. **Delete a task** (e.g., task at index 0):

bash

Copy

```
curl -X DELETE -d '0' http://localhost:8080/tasks/delete
```

Summary of the CRUD Web Server:

- We created a simple **web server** that handles CRUD operations (Create, Read, Update, Delete) for tasks.
- The server uses JSON to store tasks in a file and provides endpoints for adding, listing, and deleting tasks.
- The Go net/http package makes it easy to build RESTful APIs, and Go's built-in support for JSON handling simplifies data serialization and deserialization.

This project demonstrates how to build a simple CRUD web server with Go, providing a good foundation for building more complex applications with persistent storage and RESTful APIs.

In this chapter, you built two projects:

1. A **web scraper** using Go to collect data from a website.
2. A **simple web server** with CRUD functionality to manage tasks via HTTP requests.

301

These projects demonstrate the power of Go in handling web scraping and web server development. By building these projects, you've gained practical experience with HTTP, JSON handling, file I/O, and concurrency, which are essential skills for developing web applications in Go.

Chapter 14: Next Steps and Resources for Continued Learning

14.1 Joining the Go Community: Online Forums and Meetups

As you continue to learn and grow as a Go developer, joining the Go community can be incredibly valuable. The Go community is vast, welcoming, and filled with experienced developers who are happy to share knowledge, solve problems, and help newcomers. Here are some of the best ways to connect with others and continue your learning journey.

1. Go Forums

- **Go Forums (https://forum.golang.org/):** The official Go forum is an excellent place to ask questions, discuss Go-related topics, and share experiences. It's an active space where developers from all levels participate, from beginners to experts. You can ask about specific Go features, troubleshooting, or best practices.

- **Reddit (https://www.reddit.com/r/golang/):** The Go subreddit is a vibrant community of Go enthusiasts who share tutorials, articles, and discussions. It's a good place to stay up to date with the latest news in the Go ecosystem, ask questions, and get involved in the conversation.

2. Go Meetups

Meetups are a fantastic way to network, learn from others, and participate in hands-on workshops. They provide the opportunity to connect with Go developers in your local area and stay up-to-date on best practices.

- **Meetup.com (https://www.meetup.com/topics/golang/)**: Search for Go-related meetups in your city or online. Many Go meetups offer events where you can network, collaborate on projects, and listen to talks from industry professionals. Whether you're a beginner or an experienced developer, meetups can help you deepen your understanding of Go.

- **GopherCon (https://www.gophercon.com/)**: GopherCon is the largest annual Go conference, and it's an incredible opportunity for Go developers to come together, learn from experts, and discuss the future of Go. Even if you can't attend in person, there are often virtual options, as well as recorded sessions available after the event.

3. Go Slack Channels and Discord Servers

- **Go Slack (https://invite.slack.golangbridge.org/)**: GoBridge hosts a Slack workspace where Go developers from around the world connect. It's a great place to chat about Go programming, share ideas, ask questions, and collaborate on projects. GoBridge's Slack is especially welcoming to underrepresented groups in tech.

- **Go Community on Discord**: Some communities host Go-specific channels on Discord where you can talk with other Go developers in real-time. These channels often have dedicated spaces for learning, sharing projects, and discussing Go-related topics.

4. Go Twitter

- **#golang (https://twitter.com/hashtag/golang)**: Twitter is another place where the Go community shares news, blogs, and tips. Follow the official Go Twitter account (@golang) as well as prominent Go developers, and use the hashtag #golang to keep up with the latest Go updates.

5. Contributing to Open Source Projects

Contributing to Go open-source projects is one of the best ways to learn and gain experience. Platforms like **GitHub** host numerous Go projects where you can participate, report bugs, or even submit pull requests. Start by exploring some beginner-friendly repositories like:

- **Go-Projects** (https://github.com/golang/go): The official Go GitHub repository.
- **Awesome Go** (https://github.com/avelino/awesome-go): A curated list of Go frameworks, libraries, and software.

By contributing, you'll get practical experience with real-world Go code, which is invaluable for your growth as a Go developer.

14.2 Best Online Go Resources and Tutorials

Learning Go doesn't stop with books and tutorials—there are tons of resources available online to deepen your understanding, stay up-to-date, and explore new concepts. Here's a list of some of the best online Go resources for continued learning.

1. Go Documentation

The Go official documentation is the best place to start and continues to be an invaluable reference as you grow in your Go knowledge.

- **Go Docs** (https://golang.org/doc/): The official Go documentation includes in-depth tutorials, guides, and an introduction to Go for beginners.

- **A Tour of Go** (https://tour.golang.org/): This interactive tutorial walks you through Go's syntax and features in a hands-on way. It's a great resource if you want to quickly get a feel for Go's core concepts.
- **Go Wiki** (https://github.com/golang/go/wiki): This GitHub wiki is an excellent resource for learning about Go's features, design principles, and best practices.

2. Online Courses and Tutorials

There are several high-quality online courses that can help you master Go. These resources are suited for beginners to advanced learners and include video lectures, written tutorials, and interactive content.

- **Go by Example** (https://gobyexample.com/): This is a simple and comprehensive tutorial that demonstrates Go's syntax and features with examples. It's an excellent starting point for beginners and intermediate learners.
- **Exercism Go Track (https://exercism.io/tracks/go)**: Exercism offers a hands-on learning approach to Go with real-world exercises that teach concepts through practice. It's a great way to improve your skills through challenges and feedback.
- **Udemy Go Courses (https://www.udemy.com/courses/search/?q=go%20programming)**: Udemy offers several Go courses that cover a wide range of topics, from introductory Go programming to advanced Go web development and concurrency. The courses are affordable and often go on sale.
- **Pluralsight Go Path (https://www.pluralsight.com/paths/learn-go)**: Pluralsight offers a Go learning path, covering everything from basic syntax to more advanced topics such as concurrency, testing, and web frameworks.

3. Books

While online resources are fantastic, books provide a deep, structured learning experience. Some great books for learning Go include:

- **"The Go Programming Language" by Alan A.A. Donovan and Brian W. Kernighan**: This book is the Go developer's bible. It's written by two of the most renowned figures in computer science and offers a thorough, in-depth look at Go.
- **"Go Web Programming" by Sau Sheong Chang**: This book focuses on web development with Go, covering key concepts, techniques, and best practices for building robust web applications.
- **"Go in Action" by William Kennedy**: This book offers a hands-on approach to Go development and is great for developers who already have some programming experience and want to learn Go quickly.

4. Go Blog and Articles

Reading Go-related articles and blog posts can help you stay current with best practices, new features, and libraries. Some useful resources include:

- **The Go Blog** (https://blog.golang.org/): The Go blog is a great place to learn about new Go features, updates, and detailed discussions on Go's design philosophy.
- **Go Wiki** (https://github.com/golang/go/wiki/Resources): The Go Wiki has a collection of tutorials, blog posts, and resources shared by the community.
- **Medium - Go Programming** (https://medium.com/topic/go-programming-language): Many developers

write about Go on Medium, offering tutorials, real-world case studies, and tips and tricks for learning Go.

5. YouTube Channels and Videos

If you prefer visual learning, YouTube is full of channels that provide excellent Go tutorials, interviews with Go experts, and tips on becoming proficient with Go.

- **JustForFunc: Programming in Go**
  (https://www.youtube.com/c/JustForFunc): This YouTube channel provides high-quality Go tutorials and programming tips. It covers a variety of topics including Go concurrency, testing, and web development.
- **Go Lang Cafe** (https://www.youtube.com/c/GoLangCafe): Go Lang Cafe provides tutorials, discussions, and interviews with Go developers.
- **GoDoc - Go Documentation by Example**
  (https://www.youtube.com/c/GoDoc): This channel offers explanations and examples from the official Go documentation.

6. Go GitHub Repositories

Exploring popular Go GitHub repositories can give you insight into real-world applications and libraries. Some useful repositories include:

- **Go Standard Library** (https://github.com/golang/go/tree/master/src): The official Go repository includes the Go language's source code and standard library. It's a great resource for learning the inner workings of Go.
- **Awesome Go** (https://github.com/avelino/awesome-go): This is a curated list of Go frameworks, libraries, and software. It's a fantastic way to find tools for everything from web development to machine learning.

Summary of Resources for Continued Learning:

- **Go Docs**, **Tour of Go**, and **Go Wiki** for official documentation and tutorials.
- **Online courses** like **Go by Example**, **Exercism**, and **Udemy** for structured learning.
- **Books** such as *"The Go Programming Language"* and *"Go Web Programming"* for deep dives.
- **Go Blog**, **Medium**, and **YouTube** for up-to-date articles and tutorials.
- **GitHub repositories** for exploring real-world Go projects.

The Go community is vibrant and supportive, and the resources available for learning are vast. Whether you're just starting out with Go or looking to advance your skills, there are numerous ways to continue your learning journey. Engaging with the Go community through forums, meetups, and contributing to open-source projects can help you connect with like-minded developers and learn from the best. Using online tutorials, courses, and books will further solidify your understanding of Go, while exploring GitHub repositories and reading blogs will keep you updated on the latest trends and best practices. Happy coding!

14.3 Go Books for Advanced Learners

For advanced learners, Go offers a wealth of topics that can help deepen your understanding of the language. Once you have a solid grasp of Go's syntax, standard library, and basic patterns, it's time to explore more complex concepts such as concurrency, design patterns, testing, and optimization. Below are some excellent books that dive into these advanced topics:

1. "Go Programming Language" by Alan A.A. Donovan and Brian W. Kernighan

This book is a must-read for anyone looking to master Go. It provides a thorough introduction to Go's features, and then progresses to more advanced topics. Written by one of the creators of Unix (Brian W. Kernighan), it emphasizes Go's simplicity and its practical use in real-world projects.

Why it's great for advanced learners:

- Offers insights into Go's design and best practices.
- Goes into deep detail on Go's concurrency model.
- Discusses testing, profiling, and other advanced concepts.

2. "Go in Action" by William Kennedy

This book is excellent for developers who are familiar with Go and want to dive deeper into its features and advanced applications. It covers Go's concurrency model, testing, profiling, and how to design applications with Go's built-in tools.

Why it's great for advanced learners:

- Focuses on real-world Go application development.
- Helps you build scalable, high-performance applications using Go.
- Covers advanced topics like Go's memory model and networked applications.

3. "Mastering Go" by Mihalis Tsoukalos

This is a fantastic book for developers looking to advance their Go skills. It provides an in-depth look at Go's advanced features and how to leverage them to write efficient, concurrent, and highly scalable applications.

Why it's great for advanced learners:

- Detailed chapters on advanced Go features like reflection, channels, and goroutines.
- Covers Go's memory management and how to optimize it.
- Provides solutions to common challenges in building real-world systems.

4. "Go Web Programming" by Sau Sheong Chang

While this book is specifically focused on building web applications with Go, it's packed with advanced techniques and patterns that are useful for Go developers who want to specialize in web development.

Why it's great for advanced learners:

- Explains how to build scalable and maintainable web applications using Go.
- Covers advanced topics like security, middleware, and microservices.
- Includes hands-on projects to solidify your learning.

5. "Go Design Patterns" by Dmitri Shuralyov

Design patterns are a critical aspect of building scalable and maintainable software. This book discusses how to implement well-known design patterns in Go and covers Go-specific patterns that help with concurrency, error handling, and structuring your code.

Why it's great for advanced learners:

- Offers insight into Go-specific design patterns.
- Shows how to use concurrency to improve design and performance.
- Helps you understand how to write idiomatic Go code that scales.

6. "Concurrency in Go" by Katherine Cox-Buday

Concurrency is one of Go's most powerful features, and this book covers it in great depth. If you're serious about understanding Go's concurrency model and mastering goroutines, channels, and other concurrency-related features, this book is essential.

Why it's great for advanced learners:

- Focuses solely on concurrency and how to design concurrent systems in Go.
- Covers real-world concurrency challenges and their solutions.
- Provides detailed examples and exercises for building concurrent applications.

14.4 How to Keep Practicing and Building Your Skills

Becoming an expert in Go takes continuous practice, experimentation, and building projects. To continue improving your Go skills, it's essential to regularly apply what you've learned in real-world scenarios and challenge yourself with new problems. Here are some practical steps to keep advancing your Go expertise:

1. Build Real-World Projects

The best way to solidify your Go skills is by building real-world applications. These projects can help you apply Go's features in practical scenarios. Some ideas include:

- **A REST API**: Build a scalable web service with Go's net/http package and integrate with a database.
- **A Command-Line Tool**: Create a CLI tool that automates a specific task (e.g., managing files, interacting with APIs).

- **A Web Scraper**: Expand on your basic web scraping project by adding features like authentication, pagination, and data storage.
- **Microservices**: Build a set of microservices with Go, using technologies like Docker, Kubernetes, and gRPC for communication.

Building these kinds of projects will help you gain hands-on experience with Go and understand its strengths and weaknesses in real-world scenarios.

2. Contribute to Open-Source Projects

Contributing to open-source projects is an excellent way to gain practical experience while helping the Go community. By working on open-source projects, you'll learn best practices, tackle real-world problems, and receive feedback from other experienced Go developers.

3. Practice with Algorithms and Data Structures

Mastering algorithms and data structures is crucial for any software developer. Platforms like **LeetCode**, **HackerRank**, and **Codewars** offer a plethora of algorithmic challenges that you can solve using Go. These challenges will help you:

- Improve your problem-solving skills.
- Understand Go's performance characteristics.
- Practice writing efficient, scalable code.

4. Attend Go Meetups and Conferences

Participating in Go meetups, webinars, and conferences like **GopherCon** can help you stay up-to-date with the latest Go developments and expand your network. These events often feature talks by industry experts, hands-on workshops, and opportunities for collaboration.

5. Mentor Others and Share Knowledge

Teaching others is one of the best ways to deepen your understanding of Go. Consider:

- Writing blogs or tutorials about Go and sharing your knowledge with the community.
- Mentoring junior developers or participating in Go communities to help answer questions.
- Leading study groups or Go-focused workshops.

By mentoring others, you reinforce your own understanding and learn new perspectives that can improve your Go development skills.

6. Stay Updated with Go's Developments

Go is an actively evolving language, and it's important to keep up with the latest updates, tools, and features. Follow Go-related blogs, podcasts, and newsletters to stay informed about:

- New language features and updates (e.g., Go 1.18 introduced Generics).
- Popular libraries and frameworks.
- Industry trends and best practices.

Some resources include:

- **Go Blog** (https://blog.golang.org/)
- **Go Weekly** (https://www.golangweekly.com/)
- **Go Podcast** (https://www.golangweekly.com/go-podcast)

14.5 Becoming a Go Expert

Becoming an expert in Go requires a combination of theory, practice, and continuous learning. By engaging with the Go community, contributing to projects, and building real-world applications, you'll gradually gain a deeper understanding of Go's strengths and how to use it effectively.

Here's a roadmap to becoming a Go expert:

- **Learn the fundamentals**: Master Go's syntax, data structures, and basic programming patterns.
- **Tackle advanced topics**: Dive into concurrency, error handling, and Go's standard library.
- **Build projects**: Apply what you've learned by creating real-world applications that solve practical problems.
- **Engage with the community**: Join forums, attend meetups, and contribute to open-source projects.
- **Stay current**: Keep learning by reading blogs, books, and exploring the latest Go features.

By following this path, you will steadily improve your Go skills, contribute meaningfully to the Go community, and become a proficient Go developer capable of solving complex challenges with confidence.

Good luck on your journey to mastering Go!

Appendices

Appendix A: Go Cheat Sheet

This cheat sheet provides a quick reference to some of the most important and commonly used Go syntax, features, and patterns. It's designed to help you quickly look up common operations in Go.

1. Declaring Variables

go
Copy
```go
// Declaring variables with explicit type
var x int = 10

// Declaring variables with type inference
var y = 20

// Short variable declaration (inside a function)
z := 30
```

2. Control Flow

go
Copy
```go
// If statement
if x > y {
```

```go
    fmt.Println("x is greater")
} else {
    fmt.Println("x is not greater")
}

// Switch statement
switch x {
case 1:
    fmt.Println("One")
case 2:
    fmt.Println("Two")
default:
    fmt.Println("Other")
}
```

3. Loops

go
Copy
```go
// For loop (traditional)
for i := 0; i < 10; i++ {
    fmt.Println(i)
}

// Infinite loop
for {
    fmt.Println("This will run forever")
```

317

```go
}

// Range (iterating over slices or arrays)
for index, value := range array {
    fmt.Println(index, value)
}
```

4. Functions

go

Copy

```go
// Simple function
func add(a int, b int) int {
    return a + b
}

// Return multiple values
func swap(a, b int) (int, int) {
    return b, a
}

// Anonymous function
add := func(a, b int) int {
    return a + b
}
```

5. Structs and Methods

go

Copy

```go
// Struct declaration
type Person struct {
    FirstName string
    LastName  string
    Age       int
}

// Method on struct
func (p Person) fullName() string {
    return p.FirstName + " " + p.LastName
}

// Creating an instance of a struct
p := Person{FirstName: "John", LastName: "Doe", Age: 30}
```

6. Error Handling

go

Copy

```go
// Simple error handling
if err != nil {
    log.Fatal(err)
```

319

```
}
```

7. Concurrency with Goroutines

go

Copy

```
// Starting a goroutine
go func() {
    fmt.Println("This runs concurrently")
}()
```

8. Channels

go

Copy

```
// Creating a channel
ch := make(chan int)

// Sending a value to a channel
ch <- 42

// Receiving a value from a channel
value := <-ch
```

Appendix B: Go Glossary of Terms

Here are some key terms and concepts you'll encounter while learning Go:

- **Goroutines**: Lightweight threads managed by the Go runtime, used for concurrent programming.
- **Channels**: A way to communicate between goroutines, allowing data to be passed safely between them.
- **Structs**: Custom data types that group fields together, similar to objects in other languages.
- **Interfaces**: Types that define a set of methods. A type is said to implement an interface if it provides implementations for the methods declared by the interface.
- **Slice**: A flexible, dynamic array-like structure that allows for resizing and manipulation of data.
- **Array**: A fixed-size sequence of elements of the same type.
- **Map**: A built-in data structure that stores key-value pairs.
- **Defer**: A keyword that delays the execution of a function until the surrounding function returns.
- **Error Handling**: A way to report and handle error conditions in Go, typically done by returning an error type from functions.
- **Value vs Pointer Receiver**: In Go, methods can be defined with either value receivers (where the method operates on a copy of the struct) or pointer receivers (where the method operates on the struct directly).
- **Package**: A collection of Go files that can be imported into other Go programs, allowing code reuse.
- **Go Routine**: A function or method that runs concurrently with other functions in Go.

- **Channel**: A Go data structure used for communication between goroutines.
- **Nil**: A special value in Go representing an uninitialized variable (e.g., nil channels, slices, or pointers).
- **Generics**: A feature introduced in Go 1.18, allowing types to be parameterized, making functions and data structures more reusable.

Appendix C: Helpful Go Libraries and Tools

Go's ecosystem offers many libraries and tools that help with various tasks, from web development and databases to concurrency and testing. Here's a list of some useful libraries and tools to consider:

1. Web Development

- **Gin**: A web framework for Go, known for its performance and simplicity.
  - github.com/gin-gonic/gin
- **Echo**: Another web framework for building APIs and web applications.
  - github.com/labstack/echo
- **Gorilla Mux**: A powerful URL router and dispatcher for Go.
  - github.com/gorilla/mux

2. Database Libraries

- **gorm**: An Object Relational Mapper (ORM) for Go, allowing easy interaction with SQL databases.
  - github.com/jinzhu/gorm
- **go-redis**: A Redis client for Go.
  - github.com/go-redis/redis

3. Concurrency

- **goroutines**: Useful for managing and monitoring Go goroutines.
    - o   github.com/robfig/cron
- **go-chan**: A concurrency-focused library that provides additional tools for working with Go channels.
    - o   github.com/golang/go

4. Testing

- **Testify**: A toolkit with assertions, mocks, and other utilities for testing in Go.
    - o   github.com/stretchr/testify
- **GoMock**: A mocking framework for Go, useful for unit testing.
    - o   github.com/golang/mock
- **Gocheck**: A testing framework that extends the Go testing library with additional features.
    - o   gopkg.in/check.v1

5. Code Formatting and Linting

- **gofmt**: A built-in tool for formatting Go code to conform to Go standards.
    - o   go fmt (used via the command line)
- **golint**: A linter for Go, helping to enforce Go best practices and coding standards.
    - o   github.com/golang/lint
- **goreportcard**: Provides a quality report for your Go code, focusing on cleanliness, maintainability, and best practices.
    - o   https://goreportcard.com/

6. Other Helpful Libraries

- **Cobra**: A library for creating powerful command-line applications.
    - github.com/spf13/cobra
- **Goquery**: A library for web scraping, similar to jQuery, for working with HTML documents.
    - github.com/PuerkitoBio/goquery
- **Viper**: A configuration management library for handling environment variables, config files, etc.
    - github.com/spf13/viper
- **Logrus**: A structured logger for Go, useful for logging in complex applications.
    - github.com/sirupsen/logrus

7. Tools

- **GoDoc**: A tool for generating documentation for your Go code.
    - godoc.org
- **Delve**: A debugger for Go programs.
    - github.com/go-delve/delve
- **Docker**: A containerization tool that helps package Go applications for deployment.
    - https://www.docker.com/

Appendix D: Code Solutions to Exercises

Here are some solutions to the exercises you may have encountered in the book. The goal is to reinforce your learning and help you practice what you've learned.

1. Exercise: Basic Calculator

Write a simple calculator program in Go that performs basic arithmetic operations (addition, subtraction, multiplication, division).

Solution:

go
Copy

```go
package main

import "fmt"

func main() {
    var a, b float64
    var op string

    fmt.Println("Enter first number:")
    fmt.Scan(&a)
    fmt.Println("Enter second number:")
    fmt.Scan(&b)
    fmt.Println("Enter operator (+, -, *, /):")
    fmt.Scan(&op)
```

```go
    switch op {
    case "+":
        fmt.Println("Result:", a + b)
    case "-":
        fmt.Println("Result:", a - b)
    case "*":
        fmt.Println("Result:", a * b)
    case "/":
        if b == 0 {
            fmt.Println("Error: Division by zero")
        } else {
            fmt.Println("Result:", a / b)
        }
    default:
        fmt.Println("Invalid operator")
    }
}
```

2. Exercise: Fibonacci Sequence

Write a program to generate the Fibonacci sequence up to a given number.

Solution:

go
Copy
```
package main
```

```go
import "fmt"

func fibonacci(n int) {
    a, b := 0, 1
    for i := 0; i < n; i++ {
        fmt.Print(a, " ")
        a, b = b, a + b
    }
}

func main() {
    var n int
    fmt.Println("Enter a number to generate Fibonacci sequence:")
    fmt.Scan(&n)
    fibonacci(n)
}
```

3. Exercise: Reverse a String

Write a function to reverse a string.

Solution:

go
Copy
```go
package main

import "fmt"
```

```go
func reverse(s string) string {
    runes := []rune(s)
    for i, j := 0, len(runes)-1; i < j; i, j = i+1, j-1 {
        runes[i], runes[j] = runes[j], runes[i]
    }
    return string(runes)
}

func main() {
    var s string
    fmt.Println("Enter a string to reverse:")
    fmt.Scan(&s)
    fmt.Println("Reversed string:", reverse(s))
}
```

These solutions are a great way to practice fundamental Go programming concepts and ensure you understand how to apply them in real code.

This book has introduced you to the essentials of Go programming and guided you through several projects and examples. The appendices will serve as quick references for important Go syntax, libraries, and tools, and they'll provide additional learning resources to help you continue your Go journey. Keep practicing, engaging with the community, and exploring advanced topics to truly master Go!

www.ingramcontent.com/pod-product-compliance
Lightning Source LLC
LaVergne TN
LVHW051430050326
832903LV00030BD/3006